HOME AND SCHOOL ENVIRONMENT
THEIR INFLUENCE ON PERCEPTUAL STYLES

HOME AND SCHOOL ENVIRONMENT

THEIR INFLUENCE ON PERCEPTUAL STYLES

T. Kalyani Devi
Deptt. of Human Development and Family Studies
S.P. Mahila Viswavidhyalayam
TIRUPATI—517502

DISCOVERY PUBLISHING HOUSE
NEW DELHI—110 002

First Published—1997
Reprint : 2012

ISBN 81–7141–376–5

Published by :

Discovery Publishing House
4831/24, Ansari Road, Prahlad Street
Darya Ganj, New Delhi—110 002 (INDIA)
Phone : 327 92 45
Fax.: 91-11-3253475

Laser Typeset by :

Allied Computers,
Karnal (Haryana)

Printed at :
Dynamic Printers

Contents

Foreword

I have great pleasure in writing a foreword to this good work on Home and School Environment and their influence on perceptual styles of children. A lot has been talked about and written on the role of the home and school as socialising agents in the development of behaviour in children. The importance of early experiences in laying the foundations for shaping children's understanding is fairly well documented, with the epoch making work of Jean Piaget and later by many others. Though the International work is appreciably good the Indian effort in this direction is far from adequate. It is in this setting that the work of Dr. Kalyani takes on importance.

After briefing the reader about the context of the study she goes on to dwell at length on the many studies in related areas in Chapter 2. Instead of simply cataloguing the studies in each area the author has briefly summed up after reviewing the relevant studies in each area.

While describing the method and procedure she starts with an overall plan and a flowchart. She appears to have taken good care in developing tools of the study, taking care to enusre their reliability and validity. Though the sample of 240 students from the VIII, IX and X standards are restricted to Tirupati, the multi-stage random sampling would have ensured representativeness.

As part of the analysis the step-wise multiple regression was applied to assess the contribution of different Independent variables to two of the dependent variables namely field dependent/independence and impulsivity/reactivity. Though the independent variables have accounted for about a third of the variance in the dependent variables yet their contribution is important. The author has discussed in detail the implications of the findings.

As a whole, this book coming from Home scientist is a good attempt to analyze the effects of the home and school environment in determining the manner in which the information is received and processed. The study has highlighted that the stimulating and rich home and school environment (infrequently observed in children studying in quasi-Governmental Schools) plays a significant role in providing for a good perceptual style. The quality of intellectual stimulation provided by the parents in the home environment and teachers in the school environment goes a long way in ensuring efficient information processing in the child. This book has amply highlighted this aspect. As such, in a country where not many studies are carried out in this area. Dr. Kalyani's investigation assumes signficance. It is a pointer to the need for well-planned and executed studies of this kind. It would act as a remainder to the informed parent and teacher about their responsibility towards children.

Prof. P.V. Ramamurti

Dean

School of Social & Behavioural Sciences

Sri Venkateswara University

Acknowledgements

It is my great pleasure to express heartfelt gratitude to Dr. S.R. Venkatramaiah, Professor of Clinical Psychology, Dept. of Home Science, S.V. University College of Arts and Sciences, Tirupati for his able guidance, enlightening discussion and critical comments during every stage of the present investigation and presentation of the thesis.

I am thankful to Prof. Sesha Sai, Manager and Prof. Kodanda Ramanujam, Computer Division, Indian Institute of Technology, Madras who helped me in statistical analysis especially with regard to factor analysis with oblique rotations.

My thanks are due to Dr. V. Kodandarami Reddy, Reader and Dr. Balakrishna Naidu, Lecturer, Dept. of Econometrics for their help in statistical analysis.

I am especially grateful to Dr. Usha Sri, Reader, Dept. of Psychology, Sri Venkateswara University, Tirupati and presently who is working as Research Associate, University of Liver Pool, London for sending required research articles.

I specially express my thanks to the RELISER, Alert International Online Information Service for making special efforts to do computer search, and also getting articles from America.

I would like to thank M/s. Krishna Murthy, Books and Periodicals for taking special pains to supply the book entitled "Field-dependence in Psychological Theory, Research and Application, edited by Bertini from America.

I express my thanks to the Headmasters/Headmistress of selected schools for giving permission to collect data from the children. I am also thankful to the teachers and students of the selected schools for their help and cooperation.

T. Kalyani Devi

1

INTRODUCTION

Cognitive Styles

In recent years psychologists have begun to look at differences in the way human beings process information and deal with their environments. The individual differences observed in these strategies are to be called cognitive styles.

Cognitive style was first referred to as perceptual style. Cognitive style refers to a level of organization which is more general than the specific structures fundamental to perception, memory and judgement. It addresses the manner in which an individual will approach specific tasks solve problems.

Cognitive style is a term that covers the manner of perceiving or responding to the environment and it is one way in which individuals differ.

Cognitive styles are patterns of thought and behaviour. It influences learning and problem solving techniques. Sigel and Brodzinsky (1977) defined the cognitive style as an individual manner. This reflects the individual's personality or preference, nor his or her ability or intelligence. For example, when two children look at 3 different kinds of buildings, one child thinks of the use of each one and the other child looks at the buildings and notes only their ages and architectural styles.

Their responses to the buildings reflects different styles.

The development aspects of three different cognitive styles were studied by theorists. They are:

1) Field-dependence/Field-independence

2) Reflectivity/Impulsivity and

3) Categorization styles

Field-Dependence/Independence

Field-dependence/independence is defined by an individual's ability to consider an event or object separately from the context in which it occurs or appears. Highly field-independent persons will have little difficulty in considering an object or event separately from its field. Children who are field-independent can decide how to act on their own. Field-dependent children experience difficulty in locating the embedded figures. They are usually more sociable (Witkin and Goodenough, 1977). Field-independent children are more analytic and structural in their thinking, likely to be more successful in dealing with situations that relate logical analysis (Moos and Belins, 1986).

Reflectivity/Impulsivity

Reflectivity/impulsivity refers to the tendency of the person to pause and reflect on the quality of his answer in problem-solving situations, which involve moderate to high response uncertainty (Messer, 1976). Impulsive children tend to respond with the first answer which "pops into their head", as a result they are frequently incorrect. Reflective Children are more careful and detailed in their internal analysis of problems, as a result they are more likely to be correct. Research indicates that with increasing age children become more reflective, atleast through the early adolescent years. As children gain cognitive maturity, especially after the age of eleven, they are better able to answer quickly with high degree of accuracy (Salkind & Nelson 1980). The reflection/impulsivity pattern has been linked to many areas of problem-solving, academic achievement and socio-emotional behaviour, usually with the outcome that the reflective children perform more adaptively than impulsive children. Research indicates that impulsive pattern can be altered by training. It is possible to teach children to become more reflective (Messer, 1976). Although the origin of the reflection/impulsivity style is unknown, one current hypothesis that has received some support is that reflective children are more anxious than impulsive children about making mistakes. Fear of failure leads to a slowing down of response and more careful analysis of the problem, which in turn is likely to lead to increased accuracy (Kagan & Kogan, 1970).

Recognizing that I Q and verbal ability did not always account for how children attacked problems in the classroom, Jerome Kagan (Kagan, 1965; Rosman, Day, Albert and Phillips, 1964) considered whether some children might be more reflective, others impulsive. He devised the matching familiar figures test in which the child is given a standard picture of a common object with six variants, one identical and each of the other five differing in a minute detail that is not easily identified. The child who responds to the test quickly, barely scanning the figures, commits numerous errors; Kagan called this style as "impulsive". The child with a reflective style responds slowly, comparing, specific parts of the figures, and tends to make fewer errors. Children's reflection and impulsiveness become evident at age 5 or 6 and then show up in the way they handle a number of school tasks.

Impulsive children tell the first answer that comes to mind and they do not take time to consider other possibilities. They mispronounce words, substitute wrong words, omit some words but add others, and sometimes skip entire lines in their hurried progress through the passage (Kagan, 1965). Reflective children analyze visual stimuli into components and pay attention to details of a problem, whereas impulsive children focus on the total stimulus and on the total problem (Zelniker and Jeffrey, 1976). Reflective children not only spend more time on evaluating their hypotheses, but also gather more information on which to base their decisions, and they gather it more systematically than impulsive children (Messer, 1976).

Impulsive children can be taught to be more deliberate (Egeland, 1974). Scanning strategies, training children to look at all the alternatives and each component of the alternatives, are more effective in decreasing errors than are asking the children to wait before they respond or increasing their motivation to do well (Heider, 1971).

Hyperactive children, who have severe learning disabilities, and those who fail in school, are more likely to be impulsive (Messer, 1976). Impulsive children are more anxious about their overall competence (Block, Block and Harrington, 1974). Reflective children appear to be more attentive (Campbell, 1973), less aggressive (Thomas, 1971) and quicker to arrive at more advanced stages of moral development (Schleifer and Douglas, 1973). Brodzinsky (1975) found that impulsive children were spontaneous in their mirth, but reflective children understood better the humour of the situation.

Categorization Styles

Categorization styles refer to the types of groupings by means of which a person classifies or arranges stimuli. Several people will justify the grouping of the same objects according to different criteria. For Example one may say that a needle, a tack, and pin belong together "because they are all straight". Another may say "they are all used to connect two objects". Categorization styles have been subdivided into three types. A descriptive analytic style concentrates on a single obvious detail common to all the objects ("They are all straight"). The relational-contextual approach seizes on a common theme or function ("They are all used to connect two objects"). A categorical-inferential style focuses on the class of the objects (tools, fasteners, studs etc.) As the children develop cognitively, they tend to become more descriptive-analytical and less relational-contextual (Sigel and Brodzinsky, 1977).

Basic Theoretical Approaches

The Central assumption in Piaget's (1967) analysis of cognitive change was his belief that development depends upon a continuous interaction between organism and environment—an interaction which involves, on the one hand, environmental forces (people, objects, events) acting upon the child, and on the other hand, the child acting selectively upon the environment. Piaget thinks, "The human being is immersed right from birth in a social environment, which affects him just as the physical environment". Society, in a sense more than physical environment, changes the very structure of the individual because it not only compels him to recognize the facts, but also provides him with a ready-made system of signs and it imposes on him an infinite series of obligations. Piaget's position can be summarized by his acceptance of Durkheim's theorem that all social realities—values and processes—are created by men. The social and ideational world represent no entity without man. Such a world is the reflection of the socialization experienced by each individual in his cognitive development. Olson (1970) also observes that experience is absolutely essential to the development of intellectual structures, particularly experiences systematically provided by a parent or in an informal classroom.

The mechanism of intellectual progress, Piaget believes, consists of assimilation. That is, reality data (environmental stimuli) are modified to enable them to be incorporated into existing structures. Piaget sees the adaptive interaction between organism and environment as involving the complementary processes of assimilation and accommodation. Assimilation names the process whereby the organism utilizes something from the environment and incorporates it.

As the human being develops and his structural abilities for organizing new information become greater, he is able to use more complex schematha to understand the outside world. Piaget sees this development as occurring in four steps. The schematha that infants use are comparatively few and they all involve action. The infant period of learning is called sensorimotor, because infant intelligence uses the senses and bodily motion in its equilibration. A second stage begins about the time the child starts to talk. This is the preoperational period (from about 2 to 7 years of age). It is the time when, among other things, the child begins to develop symbolic images. He learns that words are symbols for objects. At the beginning of this stage especially, a child will take names so seriously that he cannot separate their literal meanings from the things they represent, or differentiate images from objects. By the end of this period, the child has learned that language is really quite arbitrary and that a name could just as easily represent one object as another.

In the next stage of concrete operations (about ages 7 to 11 years), the child begins to be able to think with some logic. He can classify things and deal with a hierarchy of classifications. A preoperational child, for example, cannot understand that a person can be both a Democrat and an American: he can deal with only one classification at a time. But a 7 year old understands that Democrats are a smaller group within the larger group of Americans. The concrete operational child still has several hurdles to go over before he thinks like an adult; the final and most important stage is the period of formal operations (beginning at ages 12 to 15 years). After this point the adolescent can imagine things contrary to fact; think realistically about the future; build ideals; and grasp metaphors which younger children cannot comprehend. After the age of 15 there are no more major developmental steps.

Bruner has applied cognitive theory to education, and he has had both a direct and an indirect influence on school curricula. Bruner is also fascinated with the process of intuition, creativity, and aesthetics. Bruner's three stages of development correspond roughly to Piaget's first three periods. In the enactive stage, like Piaget's sensorimotor stage, the infant leans through action. The iconic stage, akin to Piaget's preoperational stage, involves the development and use of imagery. And in Bruner's symbolic stage, the child uses language to relate the real and the abstract.

Environment

System theories emphasize the interaction between the developing person and the environment. According to the perspective, human development is the result of three major factors :

1. The person and what he/she brings to a particular situation or stage of development. This includes the results of experience as well as

of motivation.

2. The environment, or what is available to the individual in a particular situation or stage of life. This includes the significant context of life such as family, school and neighbourhood or community.

3. The interaction between the person and the environment.

PERSON ⟷ ENVIRONMENT

Bronfenbrenner (1979) uses the word ecology to refer to the interaction of the person and his or her social and physical setting (environment).

The ecology of human-development involves the scientific study of the progressive, mutual accomodation between an active growing human being and the settings in which the developing person lives.

According to Bronfenbrenner (1979) the following are the significant features of the above definition.

1. The developing person is viewed as a growing, active individual.

2. The interaction between the developing person and the environment is viewed as a two directional or reciprocal relationship. In other words, there is a process of mutual accomodation to which both person and environment make contributions.

3. The environment that is relevant to human development is not limited to a single, immediate setting (e.g. the home, school, or work). Rather, the ecological environment is much broader and includes immediate settings, interaction between immediate setting (e.g. the relationship between home and schools or home and work place) and larger settings, including the culture (which influence specific settings).

The environment exerts an influence on an individual every minute of every day.

Home Environment

The term "Home Environment" as such, or as a synonym of parental child rearing behaviours, has been used by many researchers working in different fields. Cohen (1979) observed that attitudes are notoriously difficult to define and measure, and the relationship between stated or measured parental attitudes and subsequent behaviour is problematic. According to Johnson and Medinnus (1969) the psychological atmosphere of a home may fall into any of the four quadrants, each of which represents one of the four general combinations: acceptance — autonomy, acceptance-control rejection-autonomy, and rejection-control.

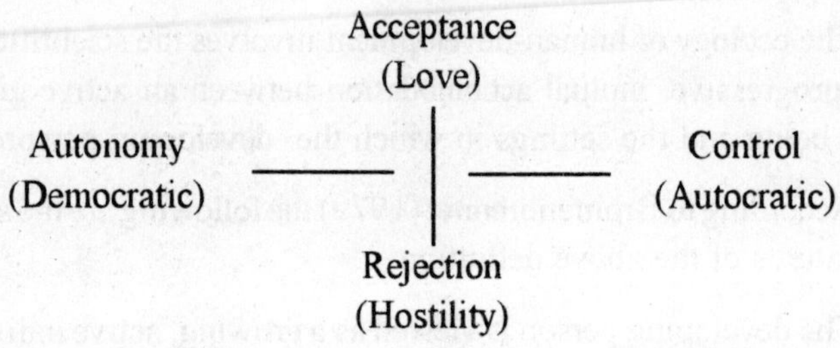

(Source : Misra, 1986)

Two characteristics recur throughout the studies of Symonds (1939), Baldwin, Kalhorn and Breese (1958), Lorr and Jenkins (1953). These are acceptance versus rejection and autonomy versus control. Grebow (1973) reports that the dimensions of parental behaviour which have been most consistently suggested as important by previous research are a) nurturance-affection and b) achievement expectations, demands and standards (Crandall, Preston & Rabson, 1960; Crandall, Katkovsky and Preston, 1960; Rosen and D'Andrade, 1959; Winterbottom, 1958).

School Environment

"School Environment" has been defined in numerous ways. Dave (1963) defined educational environment as " the conditions, processes and psychological stimuli which affect the educational achievement of the child". It refers to those forces in the environment of the learner which have the potentiality to contribute to academic development of the learner. These forces may be a part of the school or college environment, the home environment, or the environment of various other social organizations. To Hunt and Sullivan (1974), it consists of school climate as well as the teacher's approach to teaching. They consider activities as teaching methods, and institutional programmes as well as school climate to be features of the educational environment. However, this division appears to be unnecessary. Hall (1970) included the dimensions of interaction facilities, willingness to change, student's autonomy, feedback on students, instructor's contribution and task concern. Bhatnager (1977) observes: "The unique quality of the environment largely depends upon specific ways the pupils are treated in the school and classroom". He defined the concept of "Treatment Environment" as the product of the interactions between the teachers and the pupils in school situations. Perkin (1951) concludes that quality of teacher-pupil relationship in the class is the major aspect of classroom climate. Many other researchers have defined environments in terms of certain global characteristics.

School environment implies "a measure of the quality and quantity of the cognitive, creative and social support that has been available to the subjects during their school life in terms of teacher-pupil interaction". Many researchers and authors have identified the following characteristics of school environment or teacher-pupil interactions — disengagement, esprit, intimacy, product emphasis, psychophysical hindrance, alienation, control, humanized thrust, friction, cliqueness, satisfaction, speed, apathy, difficulty, favouritism, formality, direction, diversity, dis-organization, democratic, independence, enthusiasm, divergence, humour, teacher talk, home work, teaching methods, learner supportive, acceptance, problem structuring, neutral, directive, reproving, disapproving or disparaging, teacher supportive, accepts feelings, praises or encourages, aspects or uses, ideas of students, lectures, gives direction, criticizes or justifies authority, student task response, student-talk initiation and silence or confusion etc. Misra (1986) included six characteristics viz. creative stimulation, cognitive encouragement, permissiveness, control, acceptance and rejection in the school environment inventory.

An Overview

Through the available material it is observed that a major research area in perceptual styles is field-dependence/independence and reflectivity/impulsivity. Researchers have reported on some of the basic concepts and approaches and factors influencing the perceptual styles such as environment, gender, age and child rearing practices. Though there are a number of studies on influence of environment on cognitive development, they did not specifically report on home and school environment.

In the developing countries children seem to suffer a major handicap of poor environmental facility both at home and school. Both these environments largely contribute to the child's perceptual styles.

Since the different perceptual styles are seen in children, it is necessary to understand how these perceptual styles differentially influence cognitive development and consequently affect participation in scholastic programmes. Basically it is also important to find out whether these perceptual styles are determined by home and school environment. The information available, especially through cross cultural studies, is very inadequate in this area. So the present investigation has as its main aim to study the influence of home and school environment on perceptual styles of children. This study has practical relevance in planning educational programmes and modifies home and school environment. The findings of the study will help in better planning the inputs for cognitive development in children through non-formal and formal educational systems.

REVIEW OF LITERATURE

Review of Literature

The scope of the review of literature is limited to the reported studies with particular reference to the effects of home and school environment on the perceptual styles in children. More importantly, the review attempts to cover cross cultural studies written on perceptual styles, namely field-dependence/independence and reflectivity/impulsivity. It is expected that such an attempt will help in understanding the methodological issues as well as gaining insight into this theoretical concepts underlying the functions of perceptual styles in their interaction with the environment.

The review is structured into the following sub themes focussing on the problem of research as follows:

— Assessment of Home and School Environment

— Home Environment

— School Environment

— Studies on Perceptual Styles

— Studies related to Developmental and Demographic aspects of Field-dependence/Independence and Reflectivity/Impulsivity.

— Specific Effects of Socio-cultural factors on Field-dependence/independence and Reflectivity/impulsivity.

Home Environment

Home itself is a complex unit. The assessment of its psychosocial environment is not an easy matter. This is due to the complexity of the phenomenon under investigation, the number of possible approaches that can be taken, and the conceptual and methodological difficulties within each approach.

Home environment has been conceptualized as the quality of human interactions, from the point of view of the child. It includes those aspects which foster growth and development, such as family trust and confidence, sharing of ideas, making discussions, parental approval, affection, and approval of peer activities. A qualitative approach on the above line to measure home environment was developed by Watson, 1957; William and Wilson, 1961.

Child rearing attitudes, mother-child relationships and parental behaviour are important factors involved in the home environment. To assess these aspects of both normal and problematic parents, Roth, 1961; Bronfenbrenner, 1961; Mitchell, 1963; Pumroy, 1966; Rogers, 1967; Armentrout, 1975 developed various tools to measure the dimensions such as overprotection, indulgence, rejection, acceptance, nurturance, reward, punishment, deprivation of privileges, protectiveness and achievement demands. These are some of the quantitative approaches to measure home environment.

The common man's approach is to develop items and test them for their psychometric properties. Many authors used high validity and reliability tools to measure home environment.

Angenent, 1976; Scheck and Emerick, 1976 constructed questionnaires to measure how children perceive their upbringing and perception of parental supportiveness and consistency. Elardo, Bradley and Caldwell, 1975 measured the home stimulation. The other tool developed by Sharma and Chouhan, 1980, is parent child relationship scale which measures rejection Vs acceptance, carelessness Vs over protection, negligence Vs over indulgence, strong realism Vs utopian expectation, freedom Vs severe discipline. The lacunae in this approach are the lack of uniformity of content and adequate emphasis upon qualitative measures.

Another approach was developed by Bradley (1981) to assess the different aspects of the quantity and quality of the cognitive and affective support available to the child in the early environment. Perhaps, the better approach to understand the nature of environment is to conceptualize in terms of phenomenological view point, namely, the environment perceived by the child, as it was realised that emphasis given to materialistic aspects of environment does not give true information. This particular aspect is chosen by Misra (1986) who identified nine dimensions to describe home environment. They are permissiveness, control, conformity, rejection, reward, punishment, protectiveness, nurturance and deprivation of privileges.

Thus, it is apparent that measurement of children's perception of their home has attracted the attention of psychologists in various fields. However, the above mentioned tools are not culture fair. This makes them unsuitable for use in Indian context and emphasizes the importance of constructing a tool to measure children's perception of their home environment. Therefore the rationale of HEI as developed by Misra by using rigorous psychometric procedures for achieving better levels of measurement, is deemed more suitable.

School Environment

Assessment of School environment is vital in understanding its influence on the child's development. One approach that has been used in many studies is based upon students' observations (Anidon & Flanders, 1961; Cogan, 1964; Flanders, 1951; Steele, House and Kerins, 1971; Ehman, 1970). Goldberg (1968) pointed out that the validity of using students' observation as an approach for determining differential student reaction to teacher and classroom activities stems from the fact that the students observe more of the teacher's typical behaviour than is usually available to the outside observer. In addition, students are directly involved in the class room activities.

Moos (1974) thinks that perception is the primary determinant of manifest classroom behaviour. It is this perception of school environment by children that may help or hinder the realization of goals for children in general and development of cognitive styles in particular.

Measurement of perception of school environment is also one of the important factors which affect the cognitive development. To assess the school environment, learning environment inventories were developed by Walberg, 1969; Anderson, 1970; Anderson, 1971. They describe different characteristics of the classes and measure the intimacy, friction, cliqueness, satisfaction, speed, difficulty, apathy, favouritism, democratic, disorganization, satisfaction, diversity and environment. Moos and Tricket (1974) inventory measures the interpersonal relationships including student-teacher and student-student relationships, personal growth such as academic competitions among students, teacher control or innovation.

Anderson (1970) developed the pupil activity inventory to measure the frequency with which pupils engage in a number of science related activities like reading about science or television. The other inventory was developed by Silbergeld, Koenig and Manderscheid (1975). They constructed a class room atmosphere scale to assess aggression, submission, autonomy, order, affiliation, involvement spontaneity, support, variety and clarity.

Treatment environment inventory, developed by Bhatnagar (1977) measures the environmental factors like support, practical orientation, involvement, autonomy, order and organisation, programme clarity, staff control and personal problems, orientation, anger and aggressiveness. The quality of school life scale, developed by Epstein and Mc Partland (1976), measures the satisfaction with school, general well being in school, commitment to class work, interests in assignments and curricular activities and reactions to teacher and is also concerned with the quality of student-teacher relations.

A tool suitable to the Indian conditions was developed by Misra (1986) which measures the dimensions such as creative stimulation, cognitive encouragement, permissiveness, acceptance and rejection.

The above review reveals that there exists a dearth of highly reliable and valid tools that measure children's perceptions of their school environment in terms of teacher-pupil interactions. It is apparent that only a few tools were developed in India to measure school environment and there is need to develop valid tools in the Indian context. Hence, the present inventory was developed with rigorous psychometric properties.

STUDIES ON PERCEPTUAL STYLES

Studies Related to Demographic Aspects of Field-dependence/Independence and Reflectivity/Impulsivity

Field-dependence/Independence

Field-dependence/independence was introduced into the psychology by Witkin (1954) and received much attention in subsequent years. Witkin pursued the relationship between personality differences and perceptual abilities and he was the first investigator who has focussed research on sex differences in perception at all ages and he has concluded that as a general rule women are more field-dependent than men. Though the difference is not large, yet it is consistent (Witkin, 1954; Witkin & Dyk et al, 1962; Witkin, Goodenough & Karp, 1967; Witkin and Oltman 1967).

Witkin, Goodenough and Karp (1967) have investigated the developmental stability of the cognitive styles of two different samples (one tested at 8 and 13 years and the other tested at 10,14,17 and 24 years of age). They indicated the progressive increase in field-independence with age. Similar studies were also conducted by Faterson and Witkin (1970) and they discussed two longitudinal studies based on 8-13 and 10-24 year age groups. The Articulation of Body Concept (ABC) results described scores increased with age. Subjects who were designated as more field-independent at each age on the basis of EFT-RFT achieved higher score on ABC scale. Females achieved high scores than males. Oltman (1968) cross sectional data of 100 male and 100 female children of 4-13 years of age showed the significant linear increase in field-independence between the ages and of both sexes. Coates (1972) study reported significant progressive increase among the pre-school children in level of disembedding skill on the PEFT for both boys and girls.

Coates (1974a) cited nine studies based on pre-school samples, eight of which yielded higher levels of field-independence on the PEFT for females than males. For six of these eight, the difference was found to be statistically significant. Comparable findings are reported for the mean sex difference on the WPPSI block design subtest. In the data discussed by Coates, the sex difference favouring females was most pronounced at 5 years (Coates, 1974b) and had begun to reverse by 6 years. This is consistent with the CEFT standardization data for children aged 7-12 years, where mean differences although not significant, nevertheless favoured males (Karp and Konstadt, 1963). In most of the studies significant differences between the sexes on most indices of field-dependence/independence are more during the adolescent secondary school years. Kogan (1976) found no sex differences in selective college samples.

Hughes (1978) investigated the sex differences in field-dependence: Effects of unlimited time on Group Embedded Figure Test performance. GEFT was administered to the 77 undergraduates with normal time limits and 53 without time limits. Males were found to have achieved higher scores than females when the time limit was imposed and sex differences were not found in the samples who had unlimited time for tests.

Group Embedded Figures Test: Psychometric data was studied by Carter and Loo (1980) over a sample of 173 female and 93 male undergraduates of Calgary university, ranging in age from 18 to 24 years. They found that both males and females performed better in section 3 than in section 2, and both of them had greater difficulty with item 5 in section 2 than with other items in that section. The last item in section

2 and 3 showed poor performance. However, the subjects did not reach the last items in the sections within the time limit rather than that the subjects had greater difficulty with the last items. The range of scores was 0-18 for females and for males 3-18 Males were found to be more field-independent than females. The study also suggested that the norms must be brought upto date for the various populations upon which the Group Embedded Figure Test is used.

In another study, young children's academic achievement, effect of age, sex as a function of cognitive styles was examined by Saracho (1984) over a sample of 240, 1st graders and 240, 3rd graders (120 males and 120 females form each grade level). Children's Embedded Figure Test (CEFT) and comprehensive Test of Basic Skills (CTBS) were administered after 12 months. In this study cognitive styles and professional backgrounds of the teachers were also identified. Results indicated non-significant differences.

To find out the effects of age and sex differences on Group Embedded Figure Test Huss and Kayson (1985) tested 20 males and 20 females (10 of each sex were in grade 3 or 4 and 10 of each sex were in 11 or 12). Three pairs of figures were given to children to find out the simple figures which were embedded in more complex figures. They found significant age and sex differences and boys found hidden figures faster than girls, and older Children were faster than younger ones.

Bill (1987) studied the developmental trends in field-dependence among the age group of 13-21 years. Rod and Frame Apparatus Test was given to 120, 13-15 year olds, 120, 16-18 years olds and 120, 19-21 years olds and found 18 year old were more field-independent. Developmental trends indicated decreased field-dependence into adolescence and increased filed-dependence in early adult-hood.

Arrington's (1989) study reported that males were found to be more field-independent than females, but significant differences were not found among he sexes on the perceptual ability tasks. The scores of the males on GEFT seem to be higher than females.

Treating age and sex as the important variables in Group Embedded Figure Test performance, Carolina and Greenville (1988) tested the preschool children's performance. They found age differences. With regard to sex, no difference was found.

Coates 1972,1975 and Coates and Bromberg, 1973 noted that the PEFT was significantly correlated with WPPSI Vocabulary in 4 year old boys but not in girls. Significant correlations were also found between PEFT and Peabody Picture Vocabulary Test by Derman and Meissner (1972). Block and Block (1973) reported no significant correlations in either sex between PEFT and verbal intelligence measures.

Flexer and Roberge (1980) reported that the relationship between field-dependence/independence and formal operational reasoning abilities were due largely to their common overlap with I.Q.

A study on Age, Sex, Training and the Measurement of Field-dependence was undertaken by Morell (1976). Three age groups of children of 11,14 and 18 years were included in the sample. Younger group was selected from local sub-urban public school systems and the oldest group was from an introductory psychology student subject pool. Rod and Frame Test was administered to the Children in specific intervals. To improve the Rod and Frame Test performance experimental group was not only tested but also given feedback training. The results indicated the sex differences. With regard to age, ambiguous information was yielded.

Significant differences in achievement and attitudes as a function of cognitive style were found by Halpin and Peterson (1986).

Swinnen, Vandenberghe and Van Assche (1986) reported that the filed-independent children, are more successful in an unstructured learning environment than field-dependent children.

An attempt was made by Helen, Walt and Clifford (1987) to find out the cognitive learning style and achievement in mathematics. To categorize the subjects into field-dependent/independent groups, 44 high and low achieving students were given Group Embedded Figure Test. They concluded that the greater number of low achieving students were classified as filed-dependent.

Verma (1991) reported the academic achievement of both male and female children was positively significantly related with field-independent cognitive style. Field-independent children were found to have significantly higher mean academic achievement than their counter parts.

The literature, reported so far, specifically related to the filed-dependence/independence. Most of the studies showed the differences in age and sex. As the age progresses, the children become more field-independent. There was a controversy about the sex differences. Some studies reported sex differences and some did not. Low achieving students were found to be more field-dependent than high achieving students.

Reflectivity/Impulsivity

Initially reflection/impulsivity was conceptualized and operationalized by Kagan, Rosman, Day, Albert and Philips (1964).

The Matching Familiar Figure Test (MFFT) developed by Kagan et al., (1964) was a mostly used instrument to measure reflection/ impulsivity. Matching Familiar Figure Tests are available in different forms for pre-schoolers, school age children and adults. The test format involves simultaneous presentation of a figure. (e.g., boat, a pair of scissors, telephone) with four or six or eight facsimiles differing in one or more details. On each of the tests consisting of 12 items the subject is asked to select from the alternatives the one that exactly matches the standard. Time to the first response and number of errors overall are then computed. All studies with the MFFT but one report a negative correlation between response item and errors, with a median *r* of about - 48. In any given sample of subjects, the child who is above the median on MFFT response time but below the median on errors is called reflective: the child who is below the median on response time but above the median on errors is called impulsive. In early stages of his research,

Kagan used the two measures separately as indexes of reflection-impulsivity, but after that a dual index of response time and errors has been used by him.

Kagan (1965) in correlating first grade MFFT performance, found cross time correlations for latency to be. 50 for girls and .48 for boys whereas for errors, the cross time correlations were .51 for girls and .25 for boys.

The long term stability was reported in two studies (Kagan, 1965) involving administrations of the MFFT at a one year interval. The correlations for response time for one group tested in grade one and then retested in grade 2 and a second group tested in grade 3 and then retested in grade 4 ranged from .48 to over .60. For the first group the correlations for error scores were .25 for boys and .51 for girls (reported in Messer, 1970), no correlations for error scores of the grade 3 and 4 were reported.

Yardo and Kagan (1968) found correlations of 0.70 and 0.13 for the girls and boys respectively. Error scores showed low stability for both sexes (r=0.23 and 0.24).

Ward (1968) administered 2 different matching tests to kindergarten, each one, with three response alternatives made up of geometrical or meaningful figures. Results indicated that the response time on the two tests were inter-correlated (for boys .64 and for girls .57).

Kagan and Kogan (1970) defined reflection/impulsivity as concerned with degree to which the subject reflects on the validity of his solution hypothesis in problems that contain response uncertainty. The instrument that was used to assess cognitive style is the Matching Familiar Figure Test (MFFT). Each item of the test consisted of a standard and a six variants, one of which is identical to the standard. The child is requested to select the matching variant. Response latency to the first hypothesis and number of errors committed constitute the two scores of interest. They found that in school age children (approximately 6-12 years old) errors declined and response times increased with age and the relationship between the two indices is consistently negative. Longer response times are associated with a smaller number of errors and shorter response times, with larger number of errors.

Messer (1970) administered the MFFT for boys in grade 1 and gave a more difficult version to the subjects in grade 3, 2½ years later. The low, yet statistically significant, correlations for latency scores and errors on the two administrations were .31 and .33 respectively.

Adams (1972) obtained a sample of 20, 6 year old reflectives and 20 impulsives who were retested 3 weeks later with the same form of the MFFT on which they had been classified. He found that reliability coefficients ranged from 0.39 (female errors) to .58 (both sexes combined on latencies).

Ward (1973) reported that over a 3 year period, latency correlations ranged from .13 to .24 and error correlations ranged from .34 to 51.

Block, Block and Harrington (1974) have argued that there is a fundamental discrepancy between the conceptulization of reflection/ impulsivity (i.e., a decision time variable) and the measurement of the construct giving large, unspecified weight to accuracy as well as latency.

Block et al., (1974) and Ault et al (1975) both reported an internal consistency reliability coefficient for MFFT response time of .89 but lower reliabilities of .62 and 0.58 respectively, for errors.

Egeland (1974 divided and 12 MFFT forms for children and adults into three eight item forms. In a pilot study with 30 children (sample characteristics unspecified), correlations among the three tasks ranged from 0.92 to 0.98, but whether these figures applied to response time, or both was not stated.

The response of Kagan and Messer (1975) to the Block et al (1974) argument emphasized the distinction between school age and preschool age children. In the former group inverse correlations between response times and errors were presumed to be higher. Reflective children presumably take ample time to evaluate alternatives, hence making few errors; impulsive subjects presumably hurry their evaluation and thereby make numerous mistakes. In the case of preschool children, by contrast, inverse correlations between errors and latency are presumed lower, if not negligible, in magnitude, implying that the reflection/impulsivity dimension has not yet emerged or, at best is in quite rudimentary form.

The development of reflection/impulsivity and cognitive efficiency was developed by Salkind and Wright (1977). In order to illustrate analysis of MFFT performance by using I and E scores in comparison with traditional classification procedures, 223 second, third and fourth graders were selected from a small town of Kansas and administered MFFT. The age range was from 6 years 10 months to 9 years 5 months with mean age of 8 years 1 month. They were 112 males and 111 females. The children were tested individually on the standard 12 item form of the MFF, using 2 practice items. Each item has six alternatives and the child was allowed maximum of five errors for item. Latency to first response and number of errors were recorded. Alternative model of reflection/impulsivity was also presented which consisted of style dimension and an efficiency dimension, along with methodological alternatives to the traditional dependence on raw error and latency scores for classification.

Becker, Bender and Morrison (1978) testing their subjects in first grade and then again 1 year later, found cross-time correlations of .46 for latency and .36 for error.

In a study of young adolescents form age 11 to age 14, Messer and Brodzinsky (1981) reported cross-time correlations of .45 and .48 for latency and error respectively.

Engle, Klein, Kagan and Yarbrough (1977) found longer differences in performance between ages 9 and 11 years. In another study, developmental nature of reflection/impulsivity was studied over a sample of 2800 children (52.7%) males and 47.3% females) by Salkind and Nelson (1980). They found developmental trends for both males and females for mean latency and total errors. Errors begin to decrease at age 10 and then stabilize whereas latency increases upto age 10 and thereafter decreases. Age effects for errors and latency were significant. Children appear to become more reflective (fewer errors and larger latency) up through 10 years of age. For both males and females the correlations between error and latency also increase according to their age.

Reflectives were found to be more accurate than impulsives by Lawry, Welsh and Jeffrey (1983). They also reported significant age and sex differences among the children.

That reflective children are more successful in learning skills than impulsive children, was reported by Swinnen, Vandenberghe and Van Assche (1986).

Intelligence effects on reflectivity and impulsivity; ability on cognitive style were studied by Genser, Hafele and Hafele (1978). To test the reflection/impulsivity, Matching Familiar Figure Test was administered to 90, 3rd grade children. The other tests such as achievement test, intelligence test, problem-solving test and picture-game were administered. It was observed that the MFFT time variable appeared to be independent of intelligence factors combine with MFFT time. Motivation variables showed few relationships to the MFFT variables. The variables of the picture game could be predicted through intelligence factors.

A study was conducted by Brannigan, Ash and Margolis (1980) on reflection/impulsivity and children's intellectual performance over a sample of 588 eleven year old students. They administered the Matching Familiar Figure Test and WISC-R to determine if impulsives and reflectives differed on the major factor of WISC-R. Results showed reflective subjects scored significantly higher than impulsive subjects on the attention-concentration and verbal organisation sub tests. The two groups did not differ significantly on the verbal comprehension of sub tests.

Miyakawa (1980) investigated the response flexibility in cognitively impulsive children. He examined whether children's ability to control impulsive response differs with age or intelligence by administering the Matching Familiar Figure Test (MFFT) for 4th and 5th graders. For high IQ groups of 4th graders, errors on MFFT significantly decreased, latency time significantly increased. In low IQ group, errors significantly decreased without increasing on latency time. It is suggested that older impulsive response towards reflective direction were observed even in the absence of prior training.

Longitudinal consistency of Matching Familiar Figure Test performance from early childhood to preadolescence was examined by Gjerde, Block and Block (1985). The subject sample included 128 children, 64 boys and 64 girls. Children of different age groups (3,4,5 and 11 years) were administered age appropriate versions of Matching Familiar Figure Test. The results showed no significant sex differences with regard to intelligence at age 4 and 11; IQ scores are not significant for the two sexes and the latency-error correlations were all in the expected negative direction in both the sexes. The relationship between IQ and MFFT latency tends to be low in one exception. At age 11, both verbal and full scale IQ positively and strongly related to latency in boys. Relationships between IQ and MFFT error were found. In the case of girls though the verbal IQ is unrelated to MFFT error scores, negative correlation show the relationship between performance IQ and MFFT error. In the boys, verbal IQ is unrelated to MFFT error except for age 11, whereas performance IQ is consistently negatively related to MFFT scores.

The studies reviewed so far have mainly concerned themselves about the development of MFFT and also the effects of age, sex, IQ and training on MFFT. It is noticed that the small and restricted samples were taken to develop the test with less than expected levels of the measures of test-re-test reliability. Some of the authors felt that correlational analysis do not provide sufficient evidence. The most favoured technique was developed by Salkind and Wright (1977). They used a quantitative measure namely I and E score to measure reflective and impulsive subjects. Age, sex, IQ and training effects on reflectivity/impulsivity were also reported.

Specific Effects of Socio-cultural Factors on Field-dependence/Independence and Reflectivity/Impulsivity

Since Witkin, Dyk, Faterson, Goodenough and Karp (1962)

proposed the theoretical frame work of psychological differentiation, a large number of studies have been carried out on the field-dependent/ independent cognitive styles in relation to envirdnment, child rearing practices, operating in different cultures, social values, ecology and acculturation.

Wober (1967) proposed that in African culture, the proprioceptive and authority spheres are relatively more important than the visual sphere which is predominant in European and American culture. He demonstrated that Nigerian subjects, when tested with rod and frame test with a tilting chair, were better able to overcome the effects of the tilted chair when adjusting the rod to the vertical position than the American control group.

Okanji (1969) found a significant difference on rod and frame test between Nigerian adolescents of rural and urban backgrounds, under-graduates giving more differentiated performance. It has been demonstrated repeatedly that the women of any given society are more field-dependent than men (Witkin et al., 1974). Women manifest a uniformity in field-dependent cognitive style across sub-cultures and appear to support the contention that the universal cultures, expectations and the biological role of women predispose them to be relatively field-dependent.

Field-dependent subjects show a higher utilization of external social referents that aid in the removal of the ambiguity (Witkin and Goodenough, 1977). Field-dependent subjects were more attentive to social stimuli. They indicate a preferential orientation towards interpersonal relationships, thus showing interest in others; they are emotionally open and prefer to act within social situations. Witkin, Goodenough and Oltman (1979) reported Field-independent individuals experience themselves as separate and distinct from others, and they tend to rely on internal referents in interpreting the world around them. Field-dependent individuals on the other hand, have a less separate self and greater reliance on external referents, which we expect will lead to turning toward others for information, and guidance in interpreting events. Field-dependent people rely more on external frames of reference in making perceptual judgements. So in their interpersonal behaviour they rely more on the information provided by others in their social surroundings.

It was clear from Witkin's early work that field-dependence subjects rely on other people to a greater extent than do field-independent subjects (Witkin, Dyk, Faterson, Goodenough and Karp (1962). By 1977 in his review of the socio-interpersonal correlates of field-dependence, he could draw hundreds of studies in the literature to refine and extend his earlier views (Witkin, Goodenough, 1977). It became increasingly clear that field-dependent people are more socially oriented as shown for example, by greater attentiveness to interpersonal cues by a preference for being physically close to people, and by a great emotional openness in communication with others. In contrast, field-independent people have a more abstract, impersonal orientation. They are not usually very interested in others, and they show greater physical and emotional distancing. In sum, field-independent people seem to function with a greater degree of individual autonomy in their social-interpersonal behaviour.

The early studies of child rearing conducted by Witkin and his coworkers (cited by Bertini, Pizzamiglio and Wapner, 1986) concluded that if there is encouragement within the family for the child to develop separate, autonomous functioning, the child will become relatively field-independent. If there is a strong emphasis on obedience to parental authority and external control of impulses, the child will be likely to become relatively field-dependent.

Strictness and strong maternal control of the child's life characterize the child-rearing practices of societies with a relatively field-dependent modal cognitive style. Mothers are controlling, intolerant of the child's selection of its own playmates and activities, the value strict obedience and they do not generally value independence, curiosity or initiative.

Child-rearing in field-independent societies is less strict, with little use of physical punishment, and higher valuation of independence on the part of the child. Both mother and father participate directly in the care and training of children. The social and cultural forces leave their imprint on the cognitive make-up of the individual.

Most cross cultural studies of subsistence level cultures support the conclusion that hunting and gathering people tend to be more field-independent than farming people. For example, the Eskimo hunters of Arctic wastelands of North America and the Aboriginal hunters of the desert wastelands of Australia are among the most field-independent people of the world.

Socio-psychological factors influencing field-dependency have been studied by Perny (1976). He administered GEFT to 20 white and 20 black 6th graders (10 males and 10 females) in each group to study the effects of age, race and sex on field-dependence/independence in children and found significant main effects with regard to sex and race.

Giving importance to child-rearing practices, socio-economic antecedents on the Group Embedded Figure Test Performance, Albert and Howard (1977) examined the 14-15 year old high school children of racially mixed and Negro populations. Differences between ethnic groups and child rearing and SES factors determined cognitive styles.

Effects of family setting upon cognitive development of children was reviewed by Bahal and Sexena (1978) and they reported that aspects such as parental behaviour, parental child rearing practices, and parental acceptance and rejection are important factors which influence the cognitive development of the child. The factors, relevant to the child's cognitive development, included academic achievement of the parents, socio-economic status, maternal employment, family size and birth order.

Witkin (1979) reviewed the cross-cultural research on the roles of child-rearing, culture and ecology in the development of individual group and sex differences in cognitive styles. In this review three kinds of cross-cultural studies were discussed. The first group of studies examined features of child rearing implicated by western studies of the development of field-dependent or field-independent mode of functioning. The second group focussed on the role of societal or cross-cultural factors and the third group emphasised on the role of ecological factors. The studies of child-rearing practices which encourage obedience in the child and conformance to parental authority are associated with the development of a field-dependent mode of functions, whereas practices which tend to allow violation of parental authority and to encourage autonomy are associated with the development of a field-independent mode of functioning. In the first type of family setting, strictness and harshness, including physical punishment are often used as techniques to achieve conforming behaviour in the child. With regard to family structure and parental roles the type of family that is associated with field-dependence in children is one in which the mother has a dominant role in the physical and emotional care of the child though the father expects obedience and respect from his children without any direct involvement in these important areas by leaving the things to mother. Children who have polygamous and extended family structure are more commonly found to be field-independent. In accordance with these findings there is consistent evidence from a number of western studies that the sons of father-absent families have extreme reduction of parental role; as a result they are likely to be more field-independent than sons of father-present families (for example, Barclay and Cusumano, 1967; Goldstein and Peck, 1973, Wohlford and Liberman, 1970). In the third group of cross-cultural studies they found that mobile group would be relatively field-independent and sedentary groups relatively field-dependent.

Cultural influences on cognitive styles were examined by Daini and Bertini (1979) A sample of 1,188, 18-20 years olds were taken from the northern central and southern areas of Italy. Subjects were administered Human Figure Test, Group Embedded Figure Test and the Block design Test. They found that central area subjects performed at a higher level than Ss from other areas. Subjects from larger town performed better than from smaller towns. A comparative study of cognitive style in three ethnic groups was made by Ghuman (1980). He assessed the test performance of 3 groups (aged 12 years 10 months to 13 years 10 months), 50 English, 50 West Americans, and 50 Asians, who differ in cultures and socialization practices. To assess the performance, subjects were administered Group Embedded Figure Test and Spatial and Mathematical Tests. Results indicated that the performance of the Asiatics and Antilles was significantly inferior to that of the English on the GEFT. Asiatics were significantly superior to the West Indian and English groups in the mathematics test. No significant difference appeared between groups on the spatial tests, and no sex differences were found.

Majeed and Ghosh (1983) reported the relative effects of rural and urban eco-cultural influences, social class and ethnic differences on cognitive differentiation among Indian students.

Tharakan (1987) also reported the effects of rural and urban backgrounds on cognitive style over a sample of 80 adolescents (40 from urban and 40 from rural) aged 16-20 years belonging to Birooms in the plateau state of Nigeria. To study the cognitive style, GEFT was administered and the results indicated urban males are highly field-independent than urban females. When both the urban and rural boys and girls are compared, a significant difference was found between the two groups of children. Those residing in urban environment were relatively more field-independent than those in rural environments.

A study on cognitive performance and cognitive styles of young children was examined by Kalyan Masih and Curry (1987). They gave Preschool Embedded Figure Test for 31 white preschoolers and estimated the correlation of cognitive performance with cognitive style of the children and the performance differences by children's sex, age and parental income. Significant values between cognitive performance and cognitive style were reported. With regard to sex and parental income, no significant difference was found. Developmental differences caused by age of the children were noted for both cognitive performance and style.

Field-dependence/independence among Mizo children was studied by Srivastava (1989) over a sample of 120 (60 urban and 60 rural, equal number of boys and girls) of different grades (preschool grade 2 and grade 4) ranging in their age 4-5, 7-8 and 9-10 years. Subjects were administered story pictures, Embedded Figure Test (Sinhas, 1984) individually. He found significant age and sex differences. Urban children identified significantly greater number of items than their rural counter parts. Females tended to be more field-dependent, irrespective of rural/urban differences. This is due to differences in socialization and greater specialization of male and female roles with the Mizo society.

Some of the researchers reported that lower class children of 5-12 years of age are consistently more impulsive on the MFFT, as comparable samples of middle class children (Heider, 1971, Mumbauer and Miller, 1972; Schwebel, 1966, Weintraub, 1973; Zucker and Stricker, 1968). However, in the sample of 5 year olds in which MFFT response time and errors were highly correlated with IQ, the relation of social class to reflection-impulsivity disappeared when IQ was controlled (Mumbauer and Miller, 1972).

Resendiz and Fox (1985) examined the cultural influences of reflection/impulsivity in children and found that Mexican children were relatively impulsive in cognitive styles in relation to the children of other cultures such as American, Japan and Israel. Similar results were also reported by Smith and Caplan (1988).

Juliano (1977) found greater percentage of children as impulsive in lower status groups. Marjoribanks (1978) study states that family and school environments are influencing the cognitive performance. Marjoribanks (1981) also reported that lower social status Ss had high parental aspirations and low academic performance, while Sarala Paul (1987) found that cognitive styles were positively and significantly correlated with home environment.

Rath (1992) has demonstrated the deficacy of cognitive behaviour intervention in disadvantaged tribal school children. The author provided evidence that the behavioural intervention was found to foster self control and inhibitions of impulsive though actions and behaviour as indicated by MFT task scores. This study opens up the possibility of modification of impulsive cognitive styles in the case of disadvantaged children.

The important relevant studies on effects of socio-cultural factors on field-dependence/independence and reflectivity/impulsivity are presented in this section. The findings of these studies clearly show the effects of family and school environment, social class, cultural influences, urban rural backgrounds and child rearing practices on perceptual styles of children.

Overview

The following observations emerge from the review of literature presented in the preceding pages.

1. With regard to the tools to assess the Home and School environments perceived by the children, there is no uniformity or consistency among different investigations. Moreover, most of the tools were not suitable to the Indian conditions.

2. Most of the investigations in the area of field-dependence/independence and reflectivity/impulsivity were carried out on children of the preoperational period, adolescence and adulthood. There are only a handful of studies on children of formal operational period.

3. Age and sex difference were reported in most of the studies.

4. Perceptual styles and cognitive functioning are intimately related to environmental variables, social class, rural urban background and culture.

In the formulation of the present problem and the development of hypothesis for research, the above observations served as the main source of theoretical background.

The main objective of the present investigation is to study the influence of home and school environment on perceptual styles with special reference to the children of formal operational period because it is a more important stage of science education. At this stage various efforts are needed to motivate students to learn the basic concepts of science and develop their ability to apply scientific knowledge in various ways to solve various problems.

STATEMENT OF THE PROBLEM

Justification

A review of research on cognitive process reveals what has been happening in the contemporary scene. The field may be characterized in terms of its empirical focus and theoretical concerns. Cognitive process refers to the process by which the sensory input is transformed, reduced, elaborated, stored, recovered and used. The concern is with, how the individual gets, creates and uses knowledge about physical and social world. Until last decade, individual differences in the cognitive processes of perception, memory and problem-solving were viewed as reflecting differences in basic intelligence. Recently, the contribution of motivation, anxiety, conflict and attitudes to these individual differences has been explored. A major research area in perceptual styles is field-dependence/independence, a construct introduced and studied by Witkin (1962) and reflection/ impulsivity studied by Kagan (1964).

Cognitive style refers to the modes of functioning that characterize an individual's perceptual and intellectual faculties. A person with an articulated cognitive style is one who is skilled in differentiating and organizing features of his environment while a global style is the opposite. Many writers have attributed different ways of perceiving things by different individuals to such factors as the environment in which a person grows up, the gender of the individual and the child-rearing practices operating in the cultures. A number of studies on cognitive styles have been carried out in relation to social values, social consequences, child-rearing practices, ecology and acculturation.

Environments of both home and school will largely contribute to the development of child's perceptual styles. The way a person has been raised, his elementary, secondary and advanced education, his friends, his religion, his political group, his neighbourhood, all may help or hinder his cognitive or perceptual development. Environmental influence starts very early in life time i.e., during the parental development of the child. The most important part of the child's environment is the home. Family is the society in miniature, and the child is in the home and the home alone, for the first vital years of his life. When the child starts going to school, he is only there for a part of the time. He studies for only 6 hours and the rest of the time is spent by him in the home. Home is the starting point of the life of an individual and various factors of the home environment may affect or influence the perceptual styles of children.

Next to home, school is the most important experience in the process of development of the child. It is very important for development of perceptual styles. The type of school or institution in which a child is studying is said to influence perceptual styles. Role of the teacher also very much influences perceptual styles.

The Problem

Home and school environment are the most importants variables that should influence child development in general and growth of cognitive styles in particular. Systematic research into various factors of home and school environments which influence the perceptual styles is very much needed. The nature of the influence of home and school environment on perceptual styles has not been subjected to extensive studies in India, while it has been a major focus of research in the west. So, the present investigation has been taken up to determine the nature of the influence arising from home and school environment on the appearance of the specific perceptual styles among students of formal operational stage.

The following are the research questions framed for probe and study.

1. Is there any distribution bias in the quantitative measures of perceptual style in sample children ?
2. Is there any relationship between perceptual style and quality of environment ?
3. Is there any association between age and perceptual styles ?
4. Do these perceptual styles exhibit any dependencies on sex ?
5. How does intelligence relate itself to the perceptual styles ?

METHOD AND PROCEDURE

General Plan

The major objective of this research study is to see the effects of home and school environment on the perceptual styles of children. Home and school environments are operationally translated to describe various behavioural and perceived aspects within the home and school. In addition, the physical and net effective influence of these environments are also proposed to be evaluated using suitable sub-scales.

In the first stage, home environment inventory and school environment inventory will be tested on a sample of 120 subjects. The relevant psychometric properties will be established. Matching Familiar Figure Test will also be developed over a sample of 30 (depending on the Kagan's Model) on the basis of suitability of the local conditions to measure the reflectivity/impulsivity. Raven's Progressive Matrices (colour) developed by Raven (1987) will be used to measure the intelligence. To measure field-dependence/independence, Group Embedded Figure Test developed by Oltmen, Raskin and Witkin (1971) will be used.

In the second stage, the tools will administered on a final sample of 240 students. They were selected randomly from 8th, 9th and 10th standards of two private schools and two quasi-government schools in Tirupati. There were 120 boys and 120 girls.

Both the qualitative and quantitative analysis of data will be attempted. Qualitative analysis consists of evaluation of descriptive statistics for all the variables. Two series of multiple regression analyses will be done. One regression will be on field-dependence/independence, the other on the reflectivity/impulsivity. The data of regression analysis will be further treated to obtain relative contribution of the independent variables in the prediction of perceptual styles of children. The effect of demographic variables on perceptual styles will also be tested. (Fig. 1 shows the flow chart of the study design).

Tools of the Present Study

— Home Environment Inventory (HEI)

— School Environment Inventory (SEI)

— Raven's Progressive Matrices (colour)

— Tests to Measure Perceptual Styles

— Group Embedded Figure Test (GEFT)
(to measure Field-dependence/independence)

— Matching Familiar Figure Test (MFFT)
(to measure Reflectivity/Impulsivity)

The description of the various stages of inventories and tests is presented in the following pages.

Home Environment Inventory (HEI)

Home Environment Inventory consists of two parts. Part A and Part B. The items related to the perceived psycho-social environment which gives a picture of home environment are included under Part A. This inventory is constructed on the basis of Misra's (1986) inventory and it is further supported by factor analysis. Items which are related to physical aspects of HEI are included under Part B.

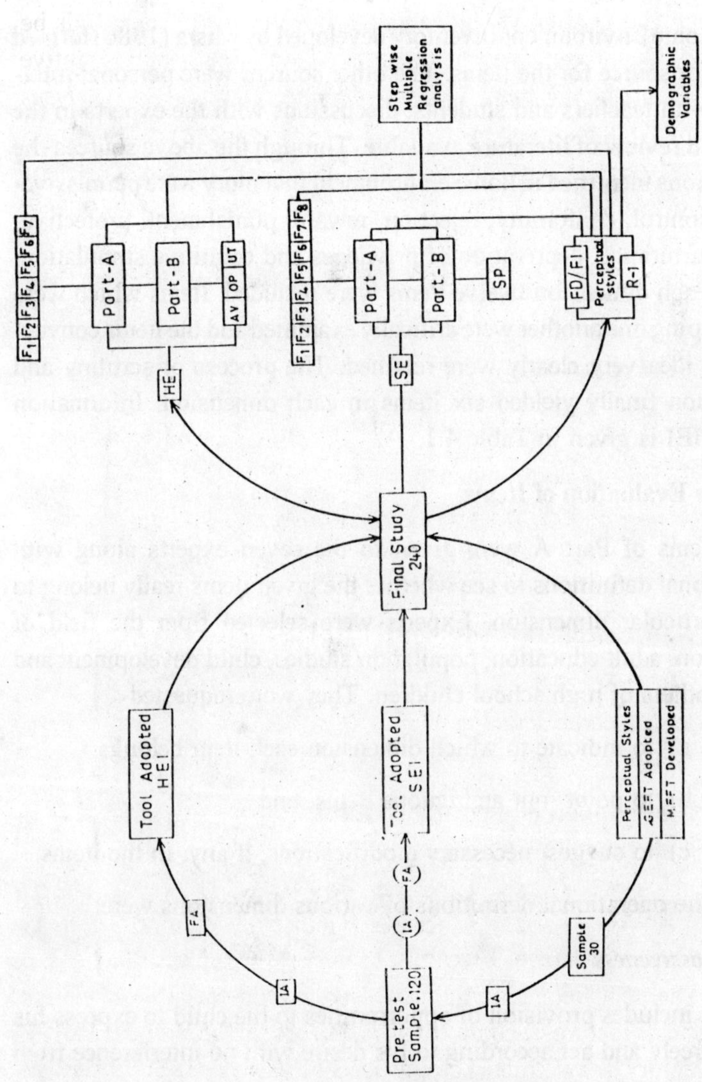

Fig. 4.1 : Study Design Flow Chart

PART A

Selection and Editing of Items

Home Environment Inventory developed by Misra (1986) formed the major source for the items. The other sources were personal interviews with teachers and students, discussions with the experts in the field and review of literature available. Through the above sources the dimensions identified in home environment inventory were permissiveness, control, conformity, rejection, reward, punishment, protectiveness, nurturance, deprivation of privileges and cognitive stimulation. Under each dimension twelve items were included. Items which were overlapping one another were critically examined and the items conveying the idea very clearly were retained. The process of scrutiny and evaluation finally yielded six items in each dimension. Information about HEI is given in Table 4.1.

Experts Evaluation of Items

Items of Part A were given to the seven experts along with operational definitions to see whether the given items really belong to that particular dimension. Experts were selected from the field of education, adult education, population studies, child development and also mothers of high school children. They were requested

a) to indicate to which dimension each item belongs;

b) to point out ambiguous items; and

c) to suggest necessary modifications, if any, in the items.

The operational definitions of various dimensions were:

1. Permissiveness

It includes provision of opportunities to the child to express his views freely and act according to his desire with no interference from parents.

2. Control

It indicates autocratic atmosphere in which many restrictions are

Table 4.1 : Information Relating to the Items of Home Environment Inventory

S.No.	Dimension	HEI Developed by Mistra			No. of items newly added	Total no. of items in the prelimi-nary form of pre-sent HEI
		Total no. of items	*No. of items accep-ted with-out modifi-cation*	*No. of items accep-ted after modifi-cation*		
	PART A					
1.	Permissiveness	10	3	3	--	6
2.	Control	10	5	1	--	6
3.	Conformity	10	5	1	--	6
4.	Rejection	10	4	--	2	6
5.	Reward	10	5	1	--	6
6.	Punishment	10	4	1	1	6
7.	Protectiveness	10	2	2	2	6
8.	Nurturance	10	3	1	2	6
9.	Deprivation of privileges	10	1	1	4	6
10.	Cognitive stimulation	--	--	--	6	6
	PART B					
1.	Availability	--	--	--	12	12
2.	Opportunity	--	--	--	12	12
3.	Utilization	--	--	--	12	12

imposed on children by the parents in order to discipline them.

3. Conformity

It indicates parents' directions, commands or orders with which child is expected to comply by action. It refers to demands to work according to parents' desires and expectations.

4. Rejection

It indicates hostile atmosphere which includes excessive criticism, invidious comparisons, refusal to pay attention, unconcern for the child's welfare and no right to express feelings.

5. Reward

It includes symbolic rewards to strengthen or increase the probability of desired behaviour.

6. Punishment

It implies the infliction of pain or discomfort, denial or removal of satisfaction to eliminate the occurrence of undesirable behaviour.

7. Protectiveness

It implies prevention of independent behaviour and prolongation of infantile care.

8. Nurturance

This includes the tendency of the parents to take care of the child's physical, psychological and social requirements so that the child grows happily. This involves all caring and supporting functions of the parents in a family.

9. Deprivation of privileges

It implies controlling children's behaviour by taking away their rights to seek love, respect, and other things which satisfy their needs.

10. Cognitive stimulation

This refers to such parental behaviour as promotes the child's awareness of its surroundings, understanding things and situations, to think and reason clearly and an overall efficiency in intelligent behaviour.

Under each dimension, an items agreed to by more than 50 per cent of the experts was included. Some items were revised and reworded and some were dropped. Finally 60 items (six for each dimension) were retained. These items were translated into Telugu and was given to language experts to examine vocabulary and meaning. Modifications and improvements suggested were done wherever necessary for clarity of the items in Telugu version. These items had three response categories, namely, many times, some times and rarely.

Pre-Try-Out

For preliminary try-out, items were arranged in a random order and administered to a sample of ten students to test its applicability. Students were encouraged to express their doubts freely. This would help us to identify the ambiguous or difficult items. After preliminary try-out necessary modification were done. Then the preliminary version of HEI was prepared.

Pre-Test

HEI preliminary version consists of a test booklet containing 60 items and a response sheet. The response categories are many times, sometimes are rarely.

One hundred and twenty six students studying 8th, 9th and 10th standards drawn from three school located in Tirupati town were selected for pre-test. Equal number of boys and girls were selected in each standard.

Table 4.2 : Standard/Sex-wise Distribution of Subjects Selected for Pre-test

Sex	Standard			Total
	8th	*9th*	*10th*	
Boys	21	21	21	63
Girls	21	21	21	63
Total	**42**	**42**	**42**	**126**

The subjects were given a test booklet and separate answer sheet. They were requested to select one of the three response categories many times, sometimes and rarely, corresponding to the item in the test booklet. Answer sheets were verified and those incomplete were removed.

Totally 120 complete answer sheets were retained for item analysis. There items were scored by assigning 3,2,1, for many times, sometimes and rarely for items answered in the favourable directions and reverse score was given to negative items. Scores obtained by each individual on various items belonging to specific dimensions were added. Then HEI Got 10 composite scores for 10 dimensions.

Item Analysis

For items analysis the answer sheets were arranged in an ascending order of scores with the lowest score on a dimension at the bottom and the highest composite score at the top. This process was repeated ten times for ten dimensions separately and each time 33 response sheets (27% of 120) were selected from either ends of the ordered sheets. These sheets represented the individuals in upper and lower criterion groups. "t" ratios were calculated for each item of every dimension to find out the discriminative power of the item. All the items were significant at 0.01 level and more.

Bi-Serial Correlation

Bi-serial correlation for items analysis was used to sharpen the scale. The validity index of each item was found by using Flagan's table to normalized bi-serial co-efficients. According to Garrett (1981) items with validity indices of 0.20 or more regarded as satisfactory. So an item with validity indices of 0.20 or more were retained.

Factor Analysis

In order to understand the factorial structure of the test, factor analysis with oblique rotations were used with a maximum of 10 factors. An items having the factor loading of 0.35 and more was included in the final form. Items which had a less than 0.35 were eliminated. There were 15 such items. In the final form there were 45 items distributed into 7 factors.

Reliability of HEI

The split half (odd and even) reliability of the inventory was computed using product movement coefficient of correlation. The reliability of the half-test was 0.66. The reliability of the half test was boosted up, using Spearman Brown Prophecy Formula; the reliability of the whole test was found to be 0.79. The value was considered high and therefore it was accepted.

Validity of the HEI

The validity of a test, or of any measuring instrument, depends upon the fidelity with which it measures what it intends to measure.

Content Validity

In the construction of HEI, items were selected on careful analysis of experts. Preliminary form was given to experts along with operational definitions. They are requested to judge which dimension each item measures. An item on which more than 50 per cent of the experts agreed was included.

Intrinsic Validity

There is a close connection between validity and reliability. This validity is given by the square root of its reliability. The intrinsic validity of HEI was $\sqrt{0.79} = 0.89$.

Item Validity

Discriminative value and validity index of each item was calculated. An item having a validity index of 0.20 or more, was included in the final form.

Factor Validity

An item, having a factor loading of 0.35 or more, was considered in the final form. There were altogether seven factors in the HEI. Each factor consists of 3 or more items.

Part B of the HEI

In the Assessment of environment the logical consideration should be normally.

1. How much of the material (Objects, things etc.) is available to the child?
2. How much of the opportunity has the child to utilize?
3. How well can the child utilize them?

Researchers evaluate the home environment by the materials and things available. Though the child is deprived of materials at home, it will have an opportunity to utilize them in friends' or neighbours' houses. So, in the assessment of physical environment availability, opportunity and utilization should be taken into consideration. Keeping these in mind, 36 questions, 12 each to three categories, availability, opportunity and utilization were formulated.

These questions were administered to the pilot study along with Part A. One mark was assigned to 'Yes' and Zero to 'No' responses. Each subject score on availability, opportunity and utilization were added separately. Item analysis was carried out three times separately for availability, opportunity was utilization. The "t" values of all these categories were significant at 0.001 level.

The Final form of HEI

HEI final form consists of a test booklet with instructions and answer sheet. Part A consists of 7 factors. The higher the score, better the home environment.

Under Part B three categories, availability, opportunity and utilization were included.

School Environment Inventory

School Environment Inventory also has to parts. Part A related to psycho-social environment. This was prepared with the help of Misra's (1986) tool and was supported by factor analysis. Part B measures the physical aspects of school environment. Silbergeld and Koeing (1975) pointed out differences in actual and perceived school environment. In fact, a teacher may be quite strict but students perceive him as permissive. They point out that perception is the primary determine of manifest classroom behaviour. In the present SEI, Part A and B together give a comprehensive behavioural, structural and phenomenological aspects of the environment.

PART A

Selection and Editing of Items

School Environment Inventory developed by Misra (1986) formed the major source for the items. The personal interviews with the teachers and students, discussions with experts in the field and review of literature available were the sources for further items.

Misra has developed SEI taking into consideration six dimensions. They are cognitive stimulation, cognitive encouragement, permissiveness, acceptance, control and rejection. The dimension influence of classmates was newly added in the present SEI and the dimension, rejection, was removed because it was felt that the negative angle of acceptance implies rejection. The items which were more suitable were selected from the dimensions of acceptance and rejection of SEI developed by Misra. This was included under the dimension of acceptance in the present SEI.

The present SEI consists of two parts: A and B. Under each dimension of Part A, twelve items were written initially. Each of these items were read and evaluated carefully for language, clarity and logical validity. The items which were considered poor were not added. The process of scrutiny and evaluation finally yielded 10 items in each dimension (information about SEI is given in Table 4.3). In Part B physical setting of school was included.

Experts Evaluation of Items

The items in Parts A were arranged at random and were given to seven experts along with operational definitions. They were from the fields of education, child development and high school teachers. They were requested to indicate

a. to which dimensions each item belongs,

Table 4.3 : Information Relating to the Items of School Environment Inventory

S.No.	Dimension	SEI Developed by Mistra			No. of items newly added	Total no. of items in the preliminary form
		Total no. of items	*No. of items accepted without modification*	*No. of items accepted after modification*		
PART A						
1.	Creative Stimulation	20	5	2	3	10
2.	Cognitive encouragement	10	2	2	6	10
3.	Permissiveness	10	3	--	7	10
4.	Acceptance	10	9	1	--	10
5.	Control	10	3	1	6	10
6.	Influence of classmates	--	--	--	10	10
PART B						
	Physical Setting	--	--	--	10	10

b. whether the items were clearly stated and easily understandable by the students of 8th standard and above and

c. to suggest necessary modification, if any.

The operational definitions are as follows:

1. Creative stimulation

This refers to such activities of the teacher as promote the child's ability to find new solutions to a problem, new modes of artistic expression and bring into existence a product new to the individual.

2. Cognitive encouragement

It implies teacher's behaviour which promotes the child's awareness of its surroundings, understanding things and solutions, to think and reason clearly and an overall efficiency in intelligent behaviour.

3. Permissiveness

It indicates a school climate in which students are provided opportunities to express their views freely.

4. Acceptance

It refers to teacher's recognition that students have the right to express feelings, to uniqueness, and to be autonomous individuals. Teachers accept the feelings of students in a non-threatening manner.

5. Control

It indicates autocratic atmosphere of the school in which general restrictions are imposed on students to discipline them.

6. Influence of classmates

It implies behaviour of other students in the class towards the child.

As per the experts' suggestions, some of the items were modified under each dimension and an item agreed to by three or more were included. Then the items were translated into Telugu and checked by the language experts. These items were arranged in random order.

Pre-try-out

The prepared preliminary form was administered to 10 students to know whether the students are following the instructions and the items. This experience gives the necessary modification to the language of the statement.

Pre-test

Pre-test was carried out over a sample of 126 students studying 8th, 9th and 10th standards of three schools located in Tirupati town. A test booklet and answer sheet was given to each student. There were three response categories, namely, many times, sometimes and rarely. The subjects were requested to mark one of the three response categories corresponding to the item in the test booklet without omitting any item.

No time limit was imposed. Incomplete answer sheets were removed. There were 6 such response sheets. Answer sheets were scored 3,2,1, marks for many times, sometimes and rarely respectively, for positive items and reverse score was given for negative items. Scores obtained by each individual on various items were added. Finally SEI yielded 6 composite scores for six dimensions.

Item Analysis

Item analysis was carried out to find out the discriminative value of each item.

"t" Test

"t" ratios were calculated The items which had significant values at 0.05 level more were retained in the final form. Items which were not significant were eliminated. There were 6 such items.

Bi-serial Correlation

Items whose validity indices showed more than 0.20 were included in the final form.

Factor Analysis

The scores of subjects on 60 items of SEI were computerised to carryout factor analysis (oblique rotations). Items having the factors. loadings of 0.35 and above were included in the final form. There were 50 items and were distributed into 8 factors.

Reliability of the SEI

The split-half (odd-even) reliability of the SEI was calculated by using product movement coefficient of correlation. The reliability of the half test was 0.71. This was boosted up by using Spearman Brown Prophecy Formula and the reliability of the whole test was 0.83.

Validity of the SEI

The following were the validities established for SEI.

Content Validity

The items selected for SEI were based on careful analysis of experts. The preliminary form was given to experts alongwith the operational definitions. An item which was agreed to by three or more experts was included under each dimension.

Intrinsic Validity

This is a square root of its reliability. The intrinsic validity of SEI was $\sqrt{0.83} = 0.91$

Item Validity

Validity for each item was calculated. Items which had a high discriminative power were included in the final form.

Part B of the SEI

Under Part B questions included were related to the perceived school, physical environment. Yet or No responses were given a score of 1 and 0 respectively. Score of ten questions were added to yield one composite score. The maximum score possible for physical environment was 10 and minimum 0. All the 120 answer sheets were scored and arranged in ascending order with the highest score at the top and lowest score at the bottom. Top 27 per cent and bottom 27 per cent were considered for item analysis. The "t" value of physical environment was 14.55 which was significant at 0.001 level.

The Final Form of SEI

The final form of SEI contained a test booklet and an answer sheet. The test booklet has two parts; Part A and Part B along with instructions. The higher the score, the better the school environment. Under Part B ten items that related to school physical setting were included.

Raven's Progressive Matrices (Colour)

It is designed to assess as accurately as possible a person's present clarity of observations and level of intellectual development. This was established by Raven (1987). The three sets of twelve problems constituting the CPM are arranged to assess the chief cognitive process of which children under 11 years of age are usually capable. The three sets together provide three opportunities for a person to develop a consistent theme of thought, and the scale of thirty six problems as a whole is designed to assess as accurately as possible, mental development upto intellectual maturity. This test is reliable and valid.

Administration and Scoring

The test was administered in groups (eight children at a time) and scored according to the instructions given in coloured progressive matrices manual by Raven 1987 edition. The scoring key consists of 3 categories A, AB and B; under each category there are 12 times. Each correct response is given a credit of 1. Total score in each category is 12. Maximum score possible on the whole test is 36.

TESTS TO MEASURE PERCEPTUAL STYLES

Group Embedded Figure Test (GEFT)

The GEFT developed by Oltman, Raskin and Witkin (1971) was adopted to measure the field-dependence/independence. The GEFT contains three sections. The first section contains 7 very simple items primarily given for practice. The second and third sections contain 9 more difficult items. This is a reliable and valid test. Each section has a specific time limit.

Administration and Scoring

This test was administered and scored as per the instructions given in Oltman, Raskin and Witkins' (1971) manual. Items of each subject are scored as per scoring key. The score is the total number of simple forms correctly traced in second and third sections. Omitted items are scored incorrect. The items in the first section are not included in the total score. The total score possible is 18.

Matching Familiar Figure Test (MFFT)

Matching familiar figuro tcst as a measure of reflectivity/impulsivity was developed by Kagan. In this test all the items take the same form, requiring the child to find which of six similar pictures exactly matches another picture.

Selection of Items

Items selected for this test were very familiar to the child and also suitable to the local conditions. Altogether 27 items were selected. They were cycle, chair, pump, shop, phone, bus, face of a boy, face of a girl, postman, policeman, carpenter, cow, elephant, horse, brinjal, lady finger, book, classroom, hospital, temple and the other seven were geometrical patterns.

Preparation of the Preliminary Test Booklet

The selected items were drawn roughly along with six alternatives for each item. These items were given to an artist to draw the pictures neatly and clearly. After these items were drawn they were checked thoroughly for clarity of the picture and to avoid mistakes in the pictures. All these 27 pictures were put in an order and made a booklet. Answer sheet was also prepared.

Pre-test

Pre-test was conducted over a sample of 30 students, studying 8th, 9th, and 10 standards.

Administered

This test was administered to each child individually in regional language for easy understanding. The child was asked to sit in front of the experimenter and was shown the items in the test booklet one by one. Before starting the test experimenter would say, "look closely at what is involved in this task. The six pictures are very alike. You have to look at several possibilities and give the correct answer". Items were showed one by one. Experimenter recorded the time taken to given the response for each item and also noted the answer given by the child for each item in the record sheet. If the child was delaying much to give the response for a particular item, the child was instructed to give the response as quickly as possible. After completion of the test 30 answer sheets were scored by giving 1 mark for each correct response. Maximum score possible for the test is 27. Then the total time taken to complete the test for each individual was also calculated.

Item Analysis

Item analysis is essential to know what percentage of the group is able to answer the item and how difficult the item is, whether the item is able to discriminate the high-scoring individual from the low-scoring individual and whether the distractors are effectively functioning. Scores were arranged in an ascending order. Top 27 per cent and bottom 27 per cent of the subjects for the item was considered for item analysis. Facility value, difficulty index and validity index were calculated for each item. An item having facility value of 0.25 to 0.85 was retained and less than 0.25 (low score) was deleted in the final booklet. Totally three items (7,17 and 18) were deleted. They were the face of a boy, a book and a classroom situation. Finally 24 items were retained in the final booklet.

Preparation of Final Test Booklet of MFFT

All these 24 items were arranged in an order of difficultly and made it into a booklet form. Once again the answer sheet was prepared.

Administration and Scoring

As per the procedure explained in the previous pages, this test was administered. Each correct response is scored by one mark. The maximum score possible is 24. Number of correct responses, wrong responses, total time taken to given correct responses and wrong responses were noted in each child's answer sheet. As per the procedure given by Salkind and Wright (1977) the score of each individual is calculated by using following formula.

$$Ii + Zei - Zli$$

Ii = Impulsivity for the ith individual

Zei = a standard score for the ith individual's total errors

Zli = a standard score for the ith individual's mean latency

Large positive I score is indicative of impulsivity and large negative I score indicate reflectivity.

Sample for Final Study

Students studying 8th, 9th and 10th standards of four high schools (2 private and 2 quasi government) of Tirupati town constituted the population. Multistage random sampling was used in selecting 240 subjects for the present study. The subjects were within the age group of 12-16 years. Of the 240 subjects, 120 were boys and 120 were girls. Table 4.4 shows the distribution of the sample.

Table 4.4 : Distribution of the Students for Final Study

Type of School	8th Standard		9th Standard		10th Standard		Total
	Boys	*Girls*	*Boys*	*Girls*	*Boys*	*Girls*	
Private							
1	10	10	10	10	10	10	60
2	10	10	10	10	10	10	60
Quasi Government							
3	10	10	10	10	10	10	60
4	10	10	10	10	10	10	60
Total	**40**	**40**	**40**	**40**	**40**	**40**	**240**

Data Collection

The tools Home Environment Inventory and School Environment Inventory were administered to the subjects after establishing proper rapport with them. The data was collected in small groups (15-20) at a time. Care was taken to avoid any monotony on the part of the subjects. The subjects were seated spaciously to avoid discussions. Raven's Progressive Matrices (colour) and Group Embedded Figure Test were also administered in small groups (8-10) at a time. Again care was taken to eliminate copying. Specific time limit was imposed on these tests. The Matching Familiar Figure Test was administered individually for each subject because each item response time has to be noted.

Statistical Analysis

The following statistical techniques were applied.

1. "t" test, bi-serial correlation, factor analysis with oblique rotations, Spearman Brown Prophecy Formula to establish validity and reliability of the tools of research
2. Mean and SDs
3. "t" test
4. Analysis of variance
5. Step-wise multiple regression analyses
6. Chi-square test

RESULTS AND DISCUSSION

In this chapter the results are presented and discussed systematically in three sections. First section deals with descriptive statistical information of various dependent and independent variables. In the second section, the effects of demographic variables on perceptual styles are discussed. The results of the step-wise multiple regression analyses are presented in the third section.

Descriptive Statistics

Field-dependence/independence and reflectivity/impulsivity are the dependent variables and the major independent variables are measures of the home and school environment.

In this section descriptive statistics of both dependent and independent variables will be presented and commented upon.

Table 5.1 shows the mean and SD of the scores of perceptual style tests.

Table 5.1 : Mean and SD of the Scores of Perceptual Style Tests

(N = 240)

	Perceptual Style Test	
	FD/FI	*R/I*
Mean	5.33	+0.01
SD	4.11	+1.69

The mean value of field-dependence/independence is 5.33 and SD is 4.11. Maximum score possible on the test is 18. The top 25% and bottom 25% cut-off points are 2 and 8 respectively. The higher the score, the more is the individual field-independent. The obtained SD value suggests that there is a greater spread (dispersion) in the scores.

With regard to reflectivity/impulsivity, the mean of I score is +0.1. The positive I score designates impulsive, while the negative indicates reflective. Even in this case, the SD is considerably high, suggesting greater dispersion in the distribution of scores.

Table 5.2 : Distribution of Sample Children by Perceptual Styles and the Mean Values

Perceptual Style	*f*	Mean
Field-dependence (<2)	75	0.91
Field-independence (>8)	61	10.89
Reflective (Negative I score)	121	–1.35
Impulsive (Positive I score)	119	+1.39

The 240 children constituted the sample. In the case of field-dependence/independence style the criterion used to identify field-dependence/independence was score corresponding to the 25th and 75th percentile points (Q1 & Q3). Therefore, the sample size was reduced to 136 (the middle 50%, 104, in the sample was excluded). The mean value obtained for field-dependence group is 0.91 whereas for field/independence group it is 10.89. The perceptual styles, reflectivity and impulsivity have the mean scores of –1.35 and +1.39 respectively. Relatively speaking, the composition of different perceptual styles in the

Table 5.3 : Proportion of Sample Children in a Four-fold Classification of the Perceptual Styles

	Perceptual Styles		
	FD	*FI*	*T*
R	0.43 (31)	0.57 (41)	1.00
I	0.65 (44)	0.35 (20)	1.00

Row proportions add up to 1.0

sample of subjects indicates that there are more field-dependent and reflective than field-independent and impulsive children.

From Table 5.3 it can be inferred that there is a significantly higher proportion of children who can be designated as field-dependent and impulsive (0.65) followed by field-independent and reflective (0.57). The χ^2 analysis also revealed that there was association between field-dependence/independence and reflectivity/impulsivity (χ^2 9.05, df 1, $P < 0.05$). The exact implications of the independent variables contributing to the perceptual styles in the socio-cultural setting, require to be further investigated.

Table 5.4 represents the mean scores of field-dependence/independence and reflectivity/impulsivity style tests of children by type of school. It is observed from the table that the mean value of field-dependence/independence is higher in private school children than in quasi-government school children. With regard to the reflectivity/impulsivity style, children in private schools obtained negative mean score (reflective) and the children in quasi-government schools got the positive mean score (impulsive).

Table 5.4 : Mean and SD of the Scores of Perceptual Style Tests by Type of School

Perceptual Style	Type of School			
	Private		*Quasi-government*	
	Mean	*SD*	*Mean*	*SD*
Field-dependence/independence	7.15	4.20	3.51	3.08
Reflectivity/Impulsivity	–0.44	1.51	+0.45	1.68

From this Table we can say that children in private schools tend to be relatively more field-independent and reflective than the children attending quasi-government schools.

Generally speaking, private school establishments provide better facilities and have greater funding to maintain qualitatively better standards. In addition, the children attending such private schools also come from better placed families in the society. In the case of quasi-government schools this is not so. Such schools generally attract children from relatively lower class families and do not have adequate financial and physical facilities compared to private schools. Because of this, it is expected that the children would differ in the expression of their perceptual styles. Our obtained results lend support to this expectation.

The mean score in respect of the perceptual styles across different categories of independent variables will be presented in the following pages.

Home and School Environment

The maximum possible score for HEI is 135. The number of items included in each factor ranges from 3 to 13. The maximum possible score for various factors ranges from 9 to 39 and the mean score from 9.41 to 26.54 (Table 5.5).

Table 5.5 : Mean and SDs of Home Environment Inventory Factors

S. No.	Variable	Max. Possible Score	Mean	SD
1.	$HEIF_1$	39	26.54	3.52
2.	$HEIF_2$	30	23.37	3.71
3.	$HEIF_3$	12	11.90	3.38
4.	$HEIF_4$	12	10.01	3.25
5.	$HEIF_5$	9	9.41	2.28
6.	$HEIF_6$	19	11.95	2.43
7.	$HEIF_7$	21	19.86	5.99

Table 5.6 provides information on school environment inventory factors. The total possible score for SEI is 150. Number of items included in each factor ranges from 3 to 9 and factor score from 7.33 to 19.02.

The mean and SDs of both independent and dependent variables are presented in Table 5.7. One to 7 are the independent variables and 8 and 9 are the dependent variables. The first variable given in this table is home environment inventory mean score (99.64). Second, third and

Table 5.6 : Mean and SDs of School Environment Inventory Factors

S. No.	Variable	Max. Possible Score	Mean	SD
1.	$SEIF_1$	24	19.02	3.08
2.	$SEIF_2$	18	12.72	1.79
3.	$SEIF_3$	21	13.60	2.52
4.	$SEIF_4$	9	7.33	2.14
5.	$SEIF_5$	27	16.24	2.58
6.	$SEIF_6$	24	18.67	3.09
7.	$SEIF_7$	18	12.12	1.85
8.	$SEIF_8$	21	13.37	2.18

Table 5.7 : Mean and SDs of Independent and Dependent Variables

S.No.	Variable	Mean	SD
1.	Home Environment Inventory Total Score (HEIT)	99.64	58.58
2.	Availability (AV)	8.18	2.57
3.	Opportunity (OP)	7.91	2.49
4.	Utilization (UT)	7.36	2.52
5.	School Environment Inventory Total Score (SEIT)	103.38	7.09
6.	Physical Setting (PS)	7.84	5.99
7.	Intelligence (RPM)	24.80	8.43
8.	Field-dependence/Independence (FD/FI)	5.33	4.11
9.	Reflectivity/Impulsivity (I score)	+0.07	1.69

fourth variables are related to the physical facilities and materials available at home. As anticipated, the results obtained are in the expected direction since there are differences in the mean scores of availability, opportunity and utilization. The mean scores of opportunity (7.91) and utilization (7.36) are lower than availability (8.18) and this may be better explained by parents' continuous persuasion of children to concentrate on education as it ensures their achieving better academic accomplishments in their future studies.

Looking into the school environment inventory score, it has a mean of 103.38 and SD of 7.09. With regard to physical facilities available, the maximum score is 10. The mean score obtained is 7.09. It shows that children have better physical facilities in their respective schools.

Intelligence (RPM score) is the other independent variable which has an important role in cognitive functioning. The total score on RPM is 36 and the mean score is 24.80. High score represents high intelligence.

Field/dependence/independence and reflectivity/impulsivity are treated as dependent variables. High score on GEFT indicates the field-independent and low score designates field-dependent. Negative 1 score on MFFT represents reflective, and positive 1 score is treated as impulsive.

Table 5.8 and 5.9 present the mean and SDs of Home and School Environment Inventories by type of school.

Table 5.8 : Mean and SDs of Home Environment Inventory Factors by Type of School

S. No.	Variable	Type of School			
		Private		*Quasi-Government*	
		Mean	*SD*	*Mean*	*SD*
1.	$HEIF_1$	27.42	3.17	25.66	3.63
2.	$HEIF_2$	24.17	3.53	22.56	3.71
3.	$HEIF_3$	11.51	3.36	12.29	3.35
4.	$HEIF_4$	9.77	1.93	10.24	4.15
5.	$HEIF_5$	9.23	2.27	9.59	2.27
6.	$HEIF_6$	11.96	2.24	11.23	2.54
7.	$HEIF_7$	20.08	3.06	19.63	7.89

Table 5.9 : Mean and SDs of School Environment Inventory Factors by Type of School

S. No.	Variable	Type of School			
		Private		*Quasi-Government*	
		Mean	*SD*	*Mean*	*SD*
1.	$SEIF_1$	19.83	2.90	18.22	3.04
2.	$SEIF_2$	12.79	1.54	12.65	2.01
3.	$SEIF_3$	13.73	2.49	13.48	2.55
4.	$SEIF_4$	7.50	1.86	7.17	2.38
5.	$SEIF_5$	16.53	2.17	15.94	2.89
6.	$SEIF_6$	19.43	2.64	17.90	3.32
7.	$SEIF_7$	12.83	1.63	11.41	1.79
8.	$SEIF_8$	13.86	2.19	12.88	2.06

The mean scores of all the factors of home environment inventory are higher in private schools than in quasi-government schools except factor 3 and 5. This shows that children in private schools have better home environment than in quasi-government schools.

It is observed from Table 5.9 that the mean values of all the factors of school environment inventory are higher in private schools, compared to the quasi-government schools. It indicates that children in private schools received better environment than quasi-government school children.

Table 5.10 shows the mean and SDs pertaining to independent and dependent variables of both private and quasi-government schools.

The home environment inventory mean score is 104.79 in private schools and 94.49 in quasi-government schools. With regard to the physical facilities, the mean scores of different components of availability, opportunity and utilization are observed at 9.68, 8.46 and 7.87 respectively in private schools, while the corresponding scores in quasi-

Table 5.10 : School-wise Distribution of Mean and SDs (in parentheses) of independent and dependent variables

S. No.	Type of School	N	Home Environment Inventory				School Environment Inventory		Intelli-gence	Perceptual Syles	
			Total	*AV*	*Op*	*Ut*	*Total*	*PS*		*FD/FI*	*R-I*
1.	Private	120	104.79 (82.11)	9.68 (1.75)	8.46 (2.39)	7.87 (2.57)	106.21 (6.24)	7.88 (1.90)	29.79 (5.25)	7.15 (4.20)	–0.439 (1.57)
2.	Quasi-Government	120	94.49 (8.31)	6.67 (2.37)	7.36 (2.47)	6.87 (2.37)	100.56 (6.76)	7.80 (8.25)	19.82 (8.06)	3.51 (3.08)	+0.453 (+1.68)

government schools are 6.67, 7.36 and 6.87.

From the Table`5.10 it is clear that the mean scores of home environment inventory and the mean scores of the different components of physical facilities at home are higher in private schools compared to quasi-government schools. The results thus obtained imply the existence of a good home environment for children in private schools compared to quasi-government schools. This may be due to the fact that the families with rich socio-economic background can afford an expensive educational system existing in private schools, whereas. it is contrary in the quasi-government schools.

In the case of school environment inventory score also the results have been obtained in a similar manner as is observed in the case of home environment inventory score. The school environment inventory mean score in private schools is calculated at 106.21 while it is 100.56 in quasi-government schools. The mean score of school physical setting is noted more or less similarly (7.88 and 7.80) in both the types of schools.

Intelligence, the other independent variable, has a mean score of 29.79 in private schools and 19.82 in quasi-government schools. Significant differences is observed between the children of these two types of schools with regard to intelligence. This may be due to the availability of facilities and opportunities the children have had in their homes and schools.

Cognizable differences are noticed between two types of schools in both independent and dependent variables as the mean scores of both these variables are consistently observed in the expected direction. The interpretation of the data reveals that the greater the home and school environment score, the better the environment. With regard to the field-dependence/independence style, the higher score children tend to be more field-independent and in the case of reflectivity/impulsivity style, children with negative 1 scores are designated as reflective, and positive scores as impulsive. It is thus observed from the results that the children studying in private schools are found to be more field-independent and effective than the children in quasi-government schools.

The means and SDs of different factors of home and school environment inventory by standard are furnished in Table 4.11 and 4.12 respectively.

Table 5.11 : Mean and SDs (in parentheses) of Home Environment Inventory Factors by Standard

S.No.	Variable	Standard		
		8th	*9th*	*10th*
1.	$HEIF_1$	27.19 (3.67)	25.89 (3.75)	26.54 (2.92)
2.	$HEIF_2$	22.75 (4.39)	23.47 (3.80)	23.88 (2.63)
3.	$HEIF_3$	11.76 (3.24)	12.08 (4.02)	11.86 (2.74)
4.	$HEIF_4$	10.29 (4.96)	9.79 (1.79)	9.99 (1.93)
5.	$HEIF_5$	9.41 (2.16)	9.48 (2.27)	9.34 (2.39)
6.	$HEIF_6$	11.76 (2.33)	11.76 (2.73)	11.25 (2.14)
7.	$HEIF_7$	19.94 (9.46)	19.47 (2.93)	20.16 (3.07)

There are not marked differences by standard in the mean and SDs of both home and school environment inventory factors. It is evident that the children studying 8th, 9th and 10th standards received more or less the similar type of both home and school environment.

Table 4.13 shows the mean and SDs of independent and dependent variables by standard. The marginal differences, if any, in the mean and SDs of independent variables are not observed consistently by standard except in home environment inventory score.

With regard to the dependent variables 9th class children seem to be more field-independent and reflective than 8th and 10th standard children.

Table 5.12 : Mean and SDs (in parentheses) of School Environment Inventory Factors by Standard

S.No.	Variable	Standard		
		8th	*9th*	*10th*
1.	$SEIF_1$	19.25 (2.87)	19.04 (3.53)	18.78 (2.77)
2.	$SEIF_2$	13.00 (1.84)	12.91 (1.65)	12.25 (1.79)
3.	$SEIF_3$	13.25 (2.53)	14.33 (3.37)	13.24 (2.51)
4.	$SEIF_4$	7.31 (2.31)	6.98 (1.99)	7.71 (2.05)
5.	$SEIF_5$	16.53 (2.62)	16.01 (2.85)	16.18 (2.18)
6.	$SEIF_6$	18.78 (3.45)	18.96 (2.78)	18.26 (2.85)
7.	$SEIF_7$	12.30 (1.89)	12.01 (1.90)	12.05 (1.76)
8.	$SEIF_8$	13.26 (2.18)	13.25 (2.11)	13.60 (2.23)

Tables 5.14 and 5.15 show the mean and SDs of home and school environment inventory factors by sex. It is observed from the table that the mean scores of girls in most of the factors are higher, compared to boys.

The mean scores of both independent and dependent variables of boys and girls are shown in Table 5.16. It is noticed from the table that girls have obtained higher scores than boys in availability, opportunity and school environment inventory.

With regard to intelligence scores, the performance of boys is slightly better than that of girls. When we see that perceptual styles - field-dependence/independence and reflectivity/impulsivity, boys tend to be more field-independent and reflective than girls.

Table 5.13 : Standard-wise Distribution of Mean and SDs (in parentheses) of independent and dependent variables

S. No.	Standard	N	Home Environment Inventory				School Environment Inventory		Intelligence	Perceptual Syles	
			Total	*AV*	*Op*	*Ut*	*Total*	*PS*		*FD/FI*	*R-I*
1.	8th	80	95.63 (8.21)	8.01 (2.75)	7.61 (2.66)	7.18 (2.75)	103.50 (6.83)	7.49 (1.86)	25.01 (7.86)	4.39 (3.45)	+0.0005 (1.76)
2.	9th	80	95.65 (10.12)	8.48 (2.23)	7.90 (2.31)	7.35 (2.54)	103.94 (7.46)	8.70 (9.97)	24.74 (8.75)	6.03 (4.64)	–0.119 (1.794)
3.	10th	80	107.65 (100.14)	8.05 (2.67)	8.21 (2.46)	7.60 (2.23)	102.71 (6.91)	7.34 (1.88)	24.66 (8.66)	5.58 (3.98)	+0.139 (1.48)

Table 5.14 : Mean and SDs (in parentheses) of Home Environment Inventory Factors by Sex

S.No.	Variable	Sex	
		Boys	*Girls*
1.	$HEIF_1$	26.28 (3.36)	26.79 (3.65)
2.	$HEIF_2$	23.27 (3.65)	23.46 (3.77)
3.	$HEIF_3$	11.60 (3.13)	12.20 (3.58)
4.	$HEIF_4$	9.87 (1.66)	10.14 (4.29)
5.	$HEIF_5$	9.42 (2.32)	9.39 (2.24)
6.	$HEIF_6$	11.31 (2.34)	11.88 (2.47)
7.	$HEIF_7$	19.52 (3.14)	20.20 (7.88)

Table 5.15 : Mean and SDs (in parentheses) of School Environment Inventory Factors by Sex

S.No.	Variable	Sex	
		Boys	*Girls*
1.	$SEIF_1$	18.82 (3.18)	19.23 (2.97)
2.	$SEIF_2$	12.62 (1.86)	12.82 (1.71)
3.	$SEIF_3$	13.35 (2.51)	13.86 (2.50)
4.	$SEIF_4$	7.39 (2.28)	7.28 (1.99)
5.	$SEIF_5$	16.07 (2.86)	16.41 (2.24)
6.	$SEIF_6$	18.12 (3.24)	19.23 (2.83)
7.	$SEIF_7$	12.22 (1.96)	12.02 (1.74)
8.	$SEIF_8$	13.21 (2.32)	13.53 (2.02)

Table 5.16 : Sex-wise Distribution of Mean and SDs (in parentheses) of independent and dependent variables

S. No.	Sex	N	Home Environment Inventory				School Environment Inventory		Intelli-gence	Perceptual Syles	
			Total	*AV*	*Op*	*Ut*	*Total*	*PS*		*FD/FI*	*R-I*
1.	Boys	120	102.13 (81.92)	7.98 (2.51)	7.84 (2.44)	7.97 (2.43)	102.14 (7.22)	8.02 (8.23)	24.45 (7.92)	5.65 (3.98)	–0.00025 (1.667)
2.	Girls	120	97.11 (9.16)	8.39 (2.61)	7.97 (2.54)	6.77 (2.47)	104.65 (6.73)	7.76 (1.83)	24.15 (8.88)	5.00 (4.22)	+0.014 (1.707)

Effect of Demographic and Other Variables on Perceptual Styles

Among several demographic variables, age and sex are most commonly used in social science research. In the present study type of school is also considered as one of the variables, which affects the child's perceptual styles. Intelligence is an another important variable that influences the cognitive functioning of the children.

Type of School and Perceptual Styles

The type of school that the child attends influences much the perceptual styles such as field-dependence/independence and reflectivity/impulsivity. Different schools provide different types of environment to the children. This may influence the child's perceptual styles considerably. In this study two types of schools are studied. They are private and the quasi-government. Private schools are run by the private management and the quasi-government schools by municipality.

Table 5.17 : Mean, SDs and 't' Value of Field-dependence/Independence Scores of Children by Type of School

S.No.	Type of School	N	Mean	SD	t
1.	Private	120	7.11	4.26	7.71**
2.	Quasi-government	120	3.45	2.98	

** Significant at 0.01 level

It is evident from the Table that field-dependence/independence scores are higher in private school children compared to quasi-government school children. 't' values showed significant difference at 0.01 level. Hence, it can be concluded that the children in private schools tend to be more field-independent in their perceptual styles (see Fig. 5.1).

Table 5.18 : Mean, SDs and 't' Value of Reflectivity/Impulsivity Scores of Children by Type of School

S.No.	Type of School	N	Mean	SD	t
1.	Private	120	–0.439	1.58	4.22**
2.	Quasi-government	120	+0.453	1.69	

** Significant at 0.01 level

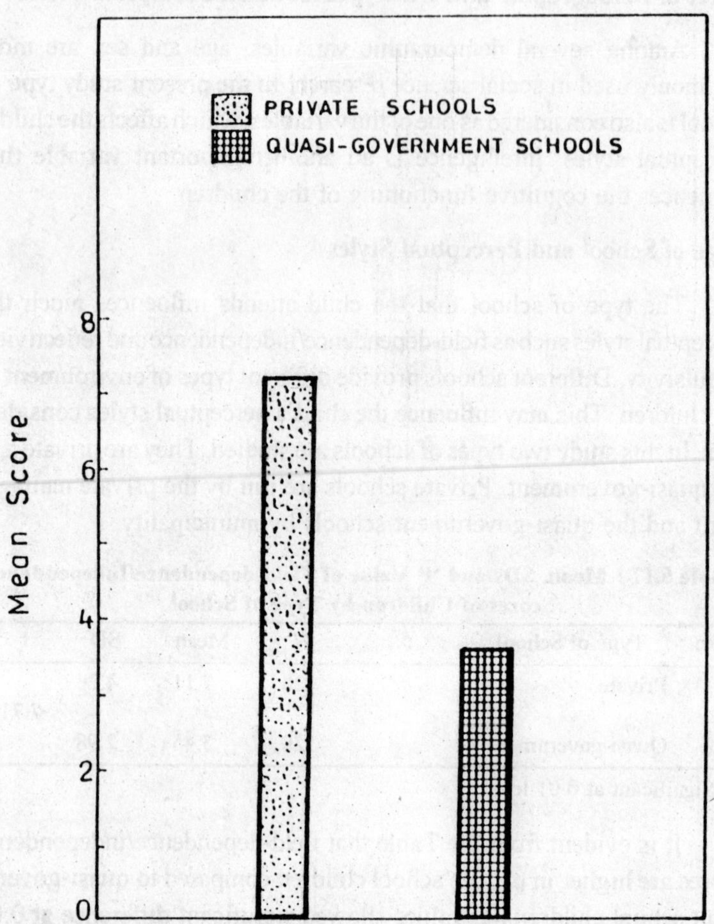

Fig. 5.1 : Bar Diagram of Field-dependence/Independence Scores of Children of Private and Quasi-Government Schools

With regard to reflectivity/impulsivity also significant difference was found between private and quasi-government school children (t=4.22, df=238, P<0.01). It is thus evident that private school children are more reflective and quasi-government school children are more impulsive. Reflectivity/impulsivity scores of children of private and quasi-government schools are shown in Fig. 5.2

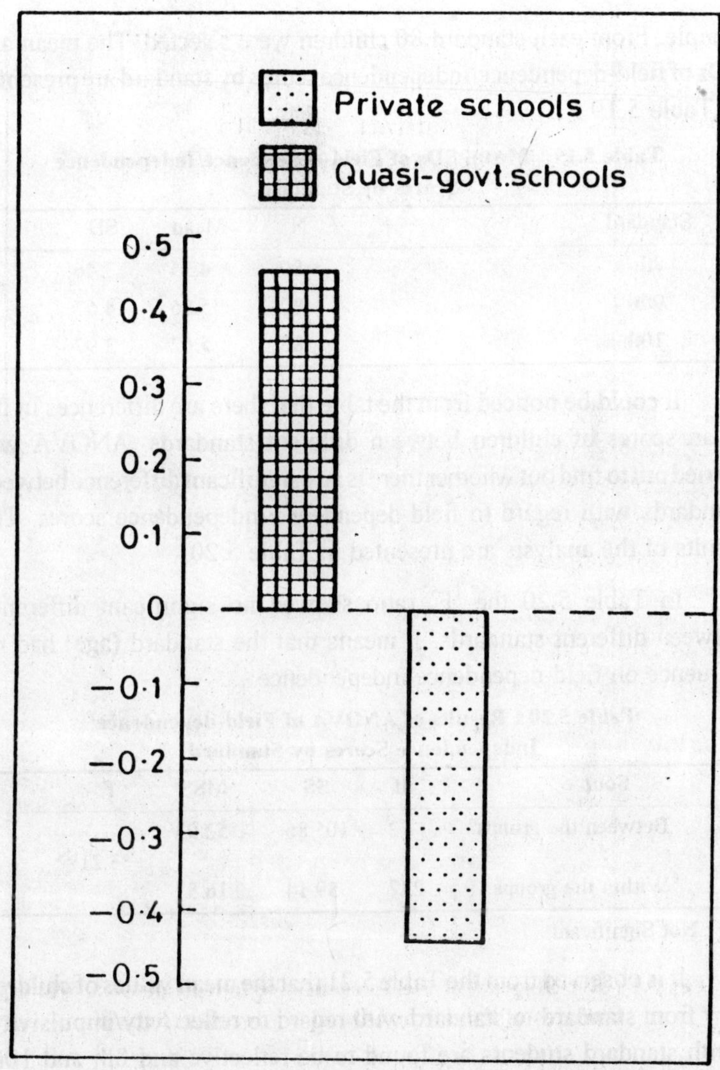

Fig. 5.2 : Reflectivity/Impulsivity Scores of Children of Private and Quasi-Government Schools

Standard and Perceptual Styles

Children studying 8th, 9th and 10th standards constituted the sample. From each standard 80 children were selected. The mean and SDs of field-dependence/independence scores by standard are presented in Table 5.19.

Table 5.19 : Mean, SDs of Field-dependence/Independence Scores by Standard

Standard	N	Mean	SD
8th	80	4.35	3.46
9th	80	5.86	4.67
10th	80	5.62	3.97

It could be noticed from the table that there are differences in the mean scores of children between different standards. ANOVA was carried out to find out whether there is any significant difference between standards with regard to field-dependence/independence scores. The results of the analysis are presented in Table 5.20.

In Table 5.20 the 'F' ratio showed no significant difference between different standards. It means that the standard (age) had no influence on field-dependence/independence.

Table 5.20 : Results of ANOVA of Field-dependence/ Independence Scores by Standard

Source	df	SS	MSS	F
Between the groups	2	105.86	52.93	3.21^{NS}
Within the groups	237	39.14	16.51	

NS : Not Significant

It is observed from the Table 5.21 that the mean values of children vary from standard to standard with regard to reflectivity/impulsivity. Ninth standard students are found to be reflective and 8th and 10th

Table 5.21 : Mean, SDs of Reflectivity/Impulsivity Scores by Standard

Standard	N	Mean	SD
8th	80	+0.0005	1.774
9th	80	–0.119	1.805
10th	80	+0.139	1.488

standard students seem to be impulsive.

Significant differences by standard are not found with regard to reflectivity/impulsivity. This indicates that the standard (age) has no significant on reflectivity/impulsivity scores of the children (Table 5.22).

Table 5.22 : Results of ANOVA of Reflectivity/ Impulsivity Scores by Standard

Source	df	SS	MSS	F
Between the groups	2	2.69	1.34	0.468^{NS}
Within the groups	237	680.88	2.87	

NS : Not Significant

Sex and Perceptual Styles

Another demographic variable studied is the sex of the subjects. Mean, SDs and 't' value of both boys and girls are presented in Table 5.23.

Table 5.23 : Mean, SDs and 't' Value of Field-dependence/Independence Scores of Children by Sex

Sex	N	Mean	SD	t
Boys	120	5.62	3.93	1.28^{NS}
Girls	120	4.94	4.25	

NS : Not Significant

The obtained results confirm that the boys and girls do not differ among themselves with regard to field-dependence/independence styles significantly. Though the obtained mean values tend to be higher than boys it is not statistically significant. Therefore it cannot be said that boys are more field-independent than girls (see Fig. 5.3). Bigelow (1971), Perny (1976), Hughes (1978), Saracho (1980), Kalyani Devi (1982), Tharakan (1987) and Arrington (1987) also reported the absence of sex differences in perceptual styles.

In the case of reflectivity/impulsivity scores shown in Table 5.24, no significant difference is found between boys and girls. Kalyan Masih

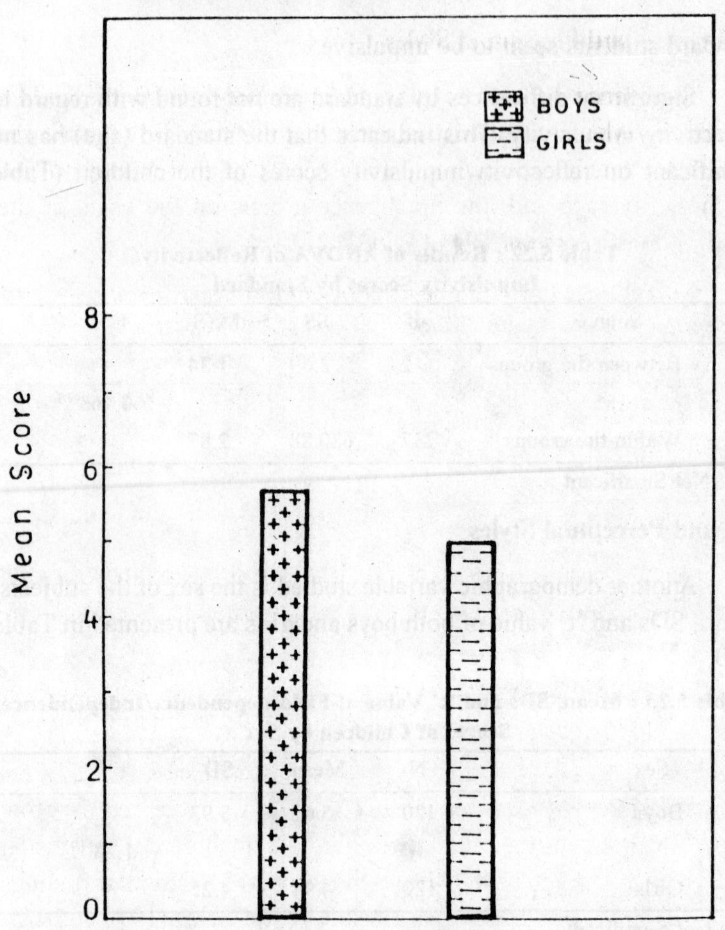

Fig. 5.3 : Bar Diagram on Field-Dependence/Independence Scores of Boys and Girls

and Curry (1987) also reported non-significant difference between boys and girls in their cognitive performance and cognitive style respectively.

Table 5.24 : Mean, SDs and 't' Value of Reflectivity/Impulsivity Scores of Children by Sex

Sex	N	Mean	SD	t
Boys	120	−0.0002	1.675	
				0.68^{NS}
Girls	120	+0.0145	1.715	

NS : Not Significant

Intelligence and Perceptual Styles

Intelligence appears to play an important role in the child's perceptual styles. An attempt is made in this study to examine the influence of intelligence on perceptual styles. Children were classified into high, average and low intelligence groups on the basis of the distribution of score on RPM (Table 5.25).

Table 5.25 : Results of ANOVA of Field-dependence/ Independence Scores by Level of Intelligence

Source	df	SS	MSS	F
Between the groups	2	1019.23	509.61	
				40.25**
Within the groups	237	3001.07	12.66	

** Significant at 0.01 level

The results of the analysis of the variance confirmed the significant main effect of intelligence on the dependent variable, namely, field-dependence/independence ($F = 40.25$, $df = 2,237$, $P < 0.01$ level). This means that the three groups of children do not constitute a homogeneous group with regard to field-dependence/independence style.

Examining the Table 5.26, it may be noticed that mean scores are consistently increasing as the level of intelligence increased. In other words, it may be inferred that, the higher the intelligence, the greater will be the tendency to be field-independent (Fig. 5.4). Similar findings were also reported by Block and Block (1973), Coates (1972 & 1975) and Coates and Bromberg (1973) and Morsla, Block and Hardy (1987).

Table 5.26 : Mean, SDs of Field-dependence/Independence Scores by Level of Intelligence

Group	N	Mean	SD
Low	59	2.66	2.61
Average	105	4.74	3.33
High	76	8.05	4.39

Low = RPM score < 19
Average = RPM score > 19 < 31. High = RPM score > 31

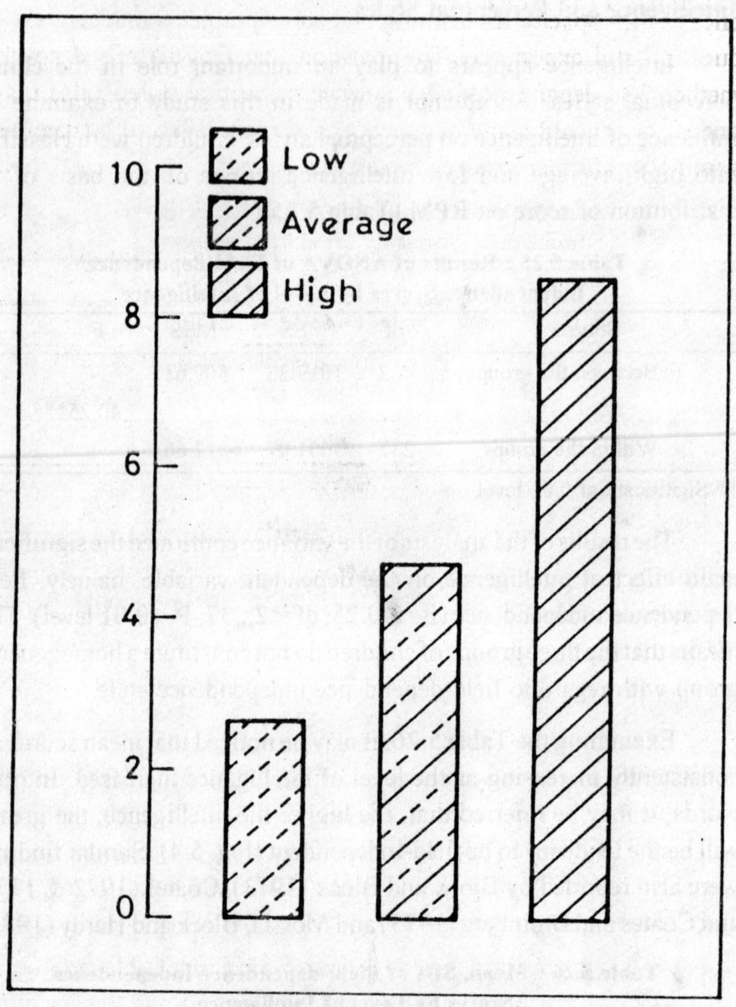

Fig. 5.4 : Field-Dependence/Independence Scores at three levels of Intelligence

The nature of intellectual functioning assessed by RPM alone in the absence of a verbal test is different from the general intelligence. This is because it involves simultaneous processing of information and correspond to what Cattell has termed fluid intolligonce. Fluid intelligence is the capacity for learning and solve problems independent of education and experience. The question that may be raised now is whether field-dependence/independence perceptual style is also independent of education and experience. This aspect has to be carefully examined by further research see Tables below).

Table 5.27 : Results of ANOVA of Reflectivity/ Impulsivity Scores by Level of Intelligence

Source	df	SS	MSS	F
Between the groups	2	43.52	21.76	
				8.06^{NS}
Within the groups	237	640.04	2.70	

NS : Not Significant

Table 5.28 : Mean, SDs of Reflectivity/Impulsivity Scores by Level of Intelligence

Group	N	Mean	SD
Low	59	+0.524	1.778
Average	105	+0.083	1.643
High	76	–0.661	1.497

With regard to the ANOVA, the effect of intelligence on reflectivity/ impulsivity style, no significant effects are observed [F = 8.05, (df=2,237) P=<0.01 level]. We cannot definitely say that intelligence has significant influence on reflectivity/impulsivity. Even though the mean values shift towards reflectivity for the higher levels of intelligence, it is rather difficult to offer any explantation to these observed findings without any further data (see Fig. 5.5). It is possible that socio-cultural factors, particularly the influence of parents and the demands of education and other systems, may have something to do with it. It is to be seen whether a measure of crystallized intelligence would show a significant effect on this perceptual style. The question again to be asked is whether or not reflectivity/impulsivity style is independent of education and experience. This aspect could not be studied in the present research.

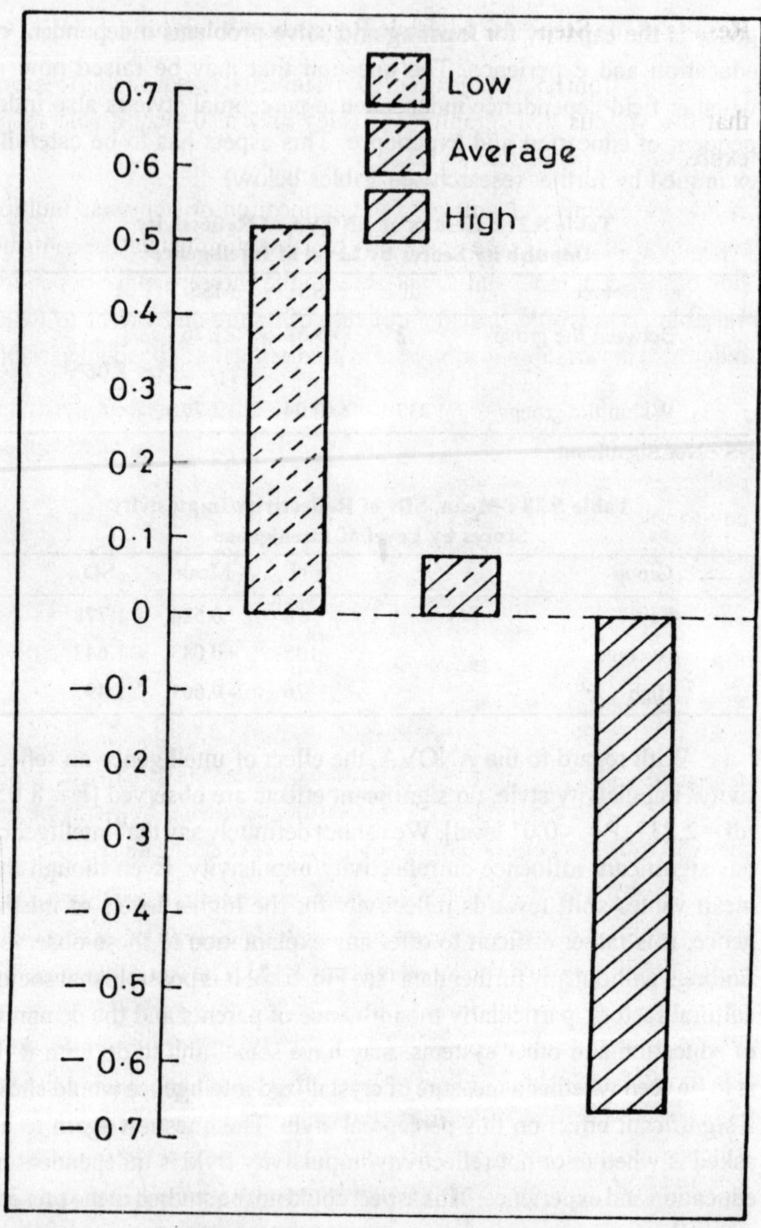

Fig. 5.5 : Reflectivity/Impulsivity Scores at Three Levels of Intelligence

Results of the Step-wise Multiple Regression Analyses

Apart from home and school environment it is reasonable to expect that the various demographic variables may also play a role in the expression of perceptual style.

One specific advantage of the application of step-wise multiple regression analyses is the possibility of valuating the relative contribution of the set of independent variables to the variance in the dependent variable. This would provide a picture of nature and extent to which independent variables are involved in predicting the dependent variable.

In the present investigation, step-wise regression analyses has been carried out on two dependent variables; Field-dependence/independence and Reflectivity/impulsivity separately. Home and school environment, type of school, standard, sex and intelligence were treated as the independent variables (Tables 5.29).

Field-dependence/independence

In this analysis, field-dependence/independence is treated as the dependent variable and home and school environment total score, type of school, standard, sex and intelligence are independent variables. Step-wise multiple regression analysis is carried out to find out the maximum possible variance in field-dependence/independence that can be explained with the help of each of the independent variables.

From the Table 5.29 it can be seen that the first variable entered in the step-wise multiple regression analysis is type of school. The multiple correlation (R) obtained is about 0.443. The value indicates that the strength of the relationship between the two variables is about 44.3%. It would also be observed from the table that F is significant at 0.01 level (F=58.07 for 1238 df). The coefficient of multiple R^2 is 0.196. This shows that 19.61% of the variance on field-dependence/independence is accounted by type of school. The standard error of the estimate is 0.478 and "t" value is 7.620, significant at 0.01 level. The constant value that would be considered in the equation at the end of the first step

Table 5.29 : Multiple (step-wise) Regression Analysis : Dependent Variable: Perceptual style-field-dependence/independence; Independence variables : Home environment inventory total score, school environment inventory total score, intelligence and demographic variables

Sl. No.	Independent Variable	R^2	R	r	Constant	b	β	Standard Error	t-value	% of variance	F-value
1	2	3	4	5	6	7	8	9	10	11	12
1.	Ty	0.196	0.443	0.443	--	–3.642	–0.443	0.478	7.620**	19.61	58.07**
2.	Ty	0.239	0.489	–0.443	5.807	–2.391	–0.291	0.578	4.139**	2.88	37.24**
	I	--	--	0.429	--	0.125	0.257	0.034	3.660**	11.04	--
3.	Ty	0.266	0.516	–0.443	–5.745	–1.823	–0.222	0.600	3.04**	9.82	28.53**
	SEI	--	--	0.331	--	0.104	0.179	0.035	2.95**	5.93	--
	I	--	--	0.429	--	0.124	0.253	0.034	3.662**	10.87	--
4.	Ty	0.283	0.532	–0.443	–7.557	–1.784	–0.217	0.595	2.999**	9.61	23.21**
	ST	--	--	0.118	--	0.658	0.131	0.279	2.363*	1.54	--
	SEIT	--	--	0.331	--	0.108	0.186	0.035	3.089*	6.16	--
	I	--	--	0.429	--	0.125	0.257	0.033	3.745**	11.01	--

R = Multiple correlation; r = Single correlation with the dependent variables; b : partial regression coefficient;
β = beta coefficient; SE = Standard Error; ** : Significant at 0.01 level
* : Significant at 0.05 level; NS : Not Significant

with which predication of field-dependence/independence would be possible is 10.792.

The general form of multiple regression equation may be given as:

$$Y=A + b_1X_1\ b_2X_2 + b_3X_3 \ldots\ldots\ldots b_nX_n$$

where Y denotes the predicated score of the dependent variable, A is a constant, $b_1, b_2, b_3 \ldots\ldots\ldots b_n$ are partial regression coefficients and $X_1, X_2, X_3 \ldots\ldots\ldots X_n$ are the scores on different independent variables. Thus the multiple regression equation at the end of this step would be written as

$$FD/FI = 10.792 + -3.642 \qquad (1)$$

The next predictor variable entered in the second step is intelligence. The multiple correlation obtained between field-dependence/independence and two independent variables viz., intelligence and type of school is 0.239. The multiple R is 0.489. F value is significant at 0.01 level ($F = 37.24$, $df = 2,237$, $P = <0.01$ level). The two variables put together could explain about 23.9% ($R^2=0.239$) of the variance in the dependent variable, field-dependence/independence. Type of school explained 12.88% of variance and intelligence I contributed 11.04% of variance.

It can be seen that by including intelligence, the contribution of type of school has been brought down from 19.61% to 12.88% due to inter correlation between the two predictor variables. The 't' values of these two variables are significant at 0.01 level. The partial regression coefficients are –2.391 and 0.125. The regression equation at this step would be

$$FD/FI = 5.807 + -2.391\ Ty + 0.125\ I \qquad (2)$$

In the third step the variable entered in the analysis is the school environment inventory total score. All these three variables put together explained 26.6% of variance on the dependent variables. School environment inventory total score accounted for 5.93% of variance. Type of school (Ty) explained 9.82% of variance and intelligence accounted for 10.87% to variance. By including school environment inventory total score in the analysis, the variance explained by type of school had come down from 12.88% to 9.82%. The variance explained by intelligence decreased from 11.04% to 10.87% due to inter-correlation prevailing among the three independent variables. The "t" values of these three independent variables; type of school, intelligence, and school environment are 3.04, 3.66 and 2.95 respectively. The values are significant at 0.01 level. The regression equation which would predict the field-dependence/independence at this step would be :

$$FD/FI = -5.745 + -1.823\ Ty + 0.174\ SEI + 0.124\ I \quad (3)$$

The variable entered as the last step in the regression analysis is standard. The multiple R is 0.532 and R^2 is 0.283 and the "t" value is significant 0.01 level on field-dependence/independence. The variance explained by the standard on field-dependence/independence is 1.54%. The regression equation at this step would be

$$FD/FI = -7.577 + -1.784\ Ty + 0.658\ ST + 0.108\ SEIT + 0.125\ I \quad (4)$$

The summary of the multiple regression analysis for the prediction of field-dependence/independence is shown in Table 5.30. The four variables-type of school, standard, school environment and intelligence - put together could explain 28.32 % of variance on field-dependence/independence. The partial regression coefficient of these variable is found to be significant. The beta coefficients are for type of school –1.784, standard 0.658, school environment inventory total score (SEIT) 0.108 and for intelligence 0.125. The multiple correlation produced by these four predictors is 0.552. The individual variance of different variables is for Ty 9.61 %, St 1.54 %, SEIT 6.16 % and I 11.01%.

Intelligence appears to be the relatively greater contributing factor in field-dependence/Independence. Next contributing factors in order, are type of school, school environment inventory total score and standard. Fig 5.6 shows the relative contribution of independent variables on field-dependence/independence.

Table 5.30 : Summary of the Multiple Regression Analysis : Dependent variable : Perceptual Style—Field-dependence/Independence; Independent variables : Home Environment Inventory, School Environment Inventory Total Score, Intelligence and Demographic Variables

Sl. No.	Independent Variable	R^2	R	r	Constant	b	β	Standard Error	t-value	% of variance	F-value
1	2	3	4	5	6	7	8	9	10	11	12
1.	Ty	0.238	0.532	–0.443	–7.577	–1.784	–0.217	0.595	2.999*	9.61	23.31**
2.	ST	--	--	0.118	--	0.658	0.131	0.279	2.363*	1.54	--
	SEIT	--	--	0.331	--	0.108	0.186	0.035	3.089*	6.16	--
	I	--	--	0.429	--	0.125	0.257	0.033	3.745*	11.01	--
	Total variance									**28.32**	.

R = Multiple correlation; r = Single correlation with the dependent variables; b : partial regression coefficient;
β = beta coefficient; SE = Standard Error ** : Significant at 0.01 level
* : Significant at 0.05 level NS : Not significant

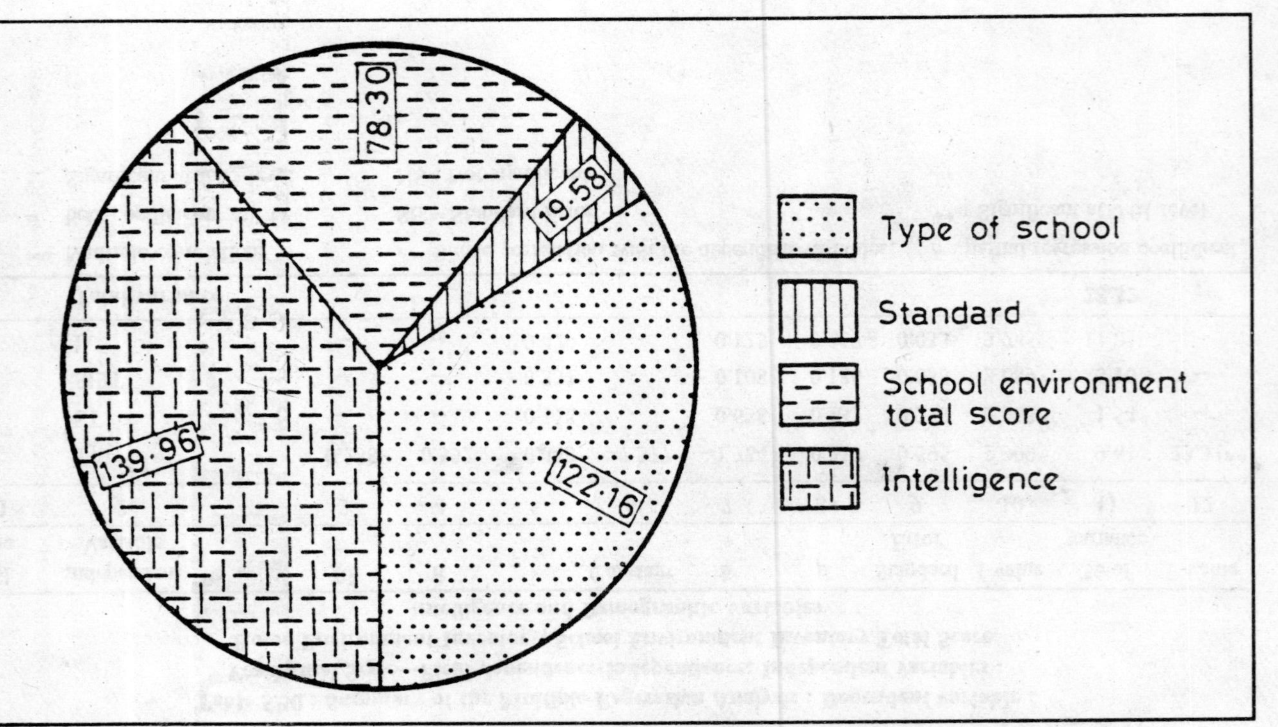

Fig. 5.6 : Relative Contribution (percentage) from independent variables to dependent variable—Perceptual Styles—Field-dependence/Independence

Reflectivity/Impulsivity

In this analysis reflectivity/impulsivity is treated as the dependent variable and home environment, school environment, standard, sex, intelligence and type of school as independent variables. Step-wise multiple regression analysis has been carried out to find out the maximum possible variance on reflectivity/impulsivity that can be explained with the help of each of the independent variables.

From the Table 5.31 it can be seen that the first variable entered in the step-wise multiple regression analysis is type of school (Ty). The multiple R obtained is 0.641. The value indicates that the strength of the relationship between the two variables is about 6.41%. It is observed from the table that F is significant at 0.01 level (F = 17.85 for 2,238 df). The coefficient of multiple R^2 is 0.070. This shows that 7.0% of the variance on reflectivity/impulsivity is accounted for by type of school. The standard error of the estimate is 0.211 and "t" value is 4.225, significant at 0.01 level. The partial regression coefficient is 0.892 and the beta coefficient is 0.264. The regression equation at this step would be

$$R/I = -1.330 + 0.892\ TY \qquad (1)$$

The next predictor variable entered ~~in~~ the second step is home environment inventory total score (HEIT). It has accounted for 1.16% of the variance. By including HEIT in the analysis, the variance explained by type of school has increased from 6.98% to 7.26 due to inter-correlation prevailing among the two independent variables. The "t" values of these two independent variables: type of school and home environment inventory score are 4.402 and 2.000 respectively. The regression equation which would predict the reflectivity/impulsivity at this step would be

$$R/I = -1.729 + 0.927\ TY + 0.004\ HEIT \qquad (2)$$

The last variable entered in the final step is intelligence. It accounts for 3.49% of variance on reflectivity/impulsivity. The regression equation which would predict the reflectivity/impulsivity at this step would

Table 5.31 : Multiple (step-wise) Regression Analysis : Dependent variable : Perceptual Style—Reflectivity/Impulsivity; Independent variables : Home Environment Inventory Total Score, School Environment Inventory Total Score, Intelligence and Demographic Variables

Sl. No.	Independent Variable	R^2	R	r	Constant	b	β	Standard Error	t-value	% of variance	F-value
1	2	3	4	5	6	7	8	9	10	11	12
1.	Ty	0.070	0.641	0.264	–1.330	0.892	0.264	0.211	4.225**	6.98	17.85**
2.	Ty	0.084	0.289	0.264	–1.729	0.927	0.275	0.211	4.402**	7.26	10.89**
	HEIT	--	--	0.196	--	0.004	0.139	0.002	2.000*	1.16	--
3.	Ty	0.097	--	0.264	–0.647	0.647	0.192	0.259	2.489*	5.06	8.44**
	HEIT	--	--	0.196	--	0.005	0.174	0.002	2.500*	1.13	--
	I	--	--	–0.250	--	0.028	–0.139	0.015	1.822^{NS}	3.49	--

R = Multiple correlation; r = Single correlation with the dependent variables; b : partial regression coefficient;

β = beta coefficient; SE = Standard Error ** : Significant at 0.01 level

* : Significant at 0.05 level NS : Not Significant

as

$$R/I = -0.647 + 0.647\ TY + 0.005\ HEIT + -0.005\ I \qquad (3)$$

The summary of the multiple regression analysis for the prediction of reflectivity/impulsivity is presented in Table 5.32. The three variables - type of school, home environment inventory total score and intelligence-put together could explain 9.68% of variance. The individual variance explained by each variable is for type of school 5.061%, home environment inventory total score 1.13% and intelligence 3.49%.

The partial regression coefficients are for type of school 0.647, home environment inventory 0.005 and for intelligence –0.028 and the beta coefficients for type of school, home environment inventory total score and intelligence are 0.192, 0.174 and –0.139 respectively.

Among the these three variables type of school (5.06%) is found to be a highly contributing factor on reflectivity/impulsivity. Next contributing factors are intelligence and home environment inventory score. Fig. 5.7 shows the relative contribution of independent variables on reflectivity/impulsivity.

DISCUSSION

Field-dependence/Independence

The multiple regression analysis has been carried out to evaluate the contribution of independent variables to the perceptual style-Field-dependence/independence. In this analysis, type of school is entered as the first step. The type of school which the child attends plays an important role in child's perceptual styles, Field-dependence/independence, because children attending private schools possess better facilities compared to the quasi-government school children. The results of the present study clearly indicated that the type of school the child attends has much influence on field/dependence/independence. Children in private schools were found to be more field/independent compared to the quasi-government school children. The type of school explained 9.61% of variance on field-dependence/independence.

Table 5.32 : Summary of the Multiple Regression Analysis : Dependent variable : Perceptual Style—Reflectivity/Impulsivity; Independent variables : Home Environment Inventory, School Environment Inventory Total Score, Intelligence and Demographic Variables

Sl. No.	Independent Variable	R^2	R	*r*	Constant	*b*	β	Standard Error	t-value	% of variance	F-value
1	2	3	4	5	6	7	8	9	10	11	12
1.	Ty	0.097	--	0.264	0.647	0.647	0.192	0.259	2.489*	5.06	8.44*
	HEIT	--	--	0.196	--	0.005	0.174	0.002	2.500*	1.13	--
	I	--	--	0.250	--	–0.028	–0.139	0.015	1.822^{NS}	3.49	--
	Total variance									9.68	

R = Multiple correlation; *r* = Single correlation with the dependent variables; *b* : partial regression coefficient;

β = beta coefficient; SE = Standard Error ** : Significant at 0.01 level

* : Significant at 0.05 level NS : Not Significant

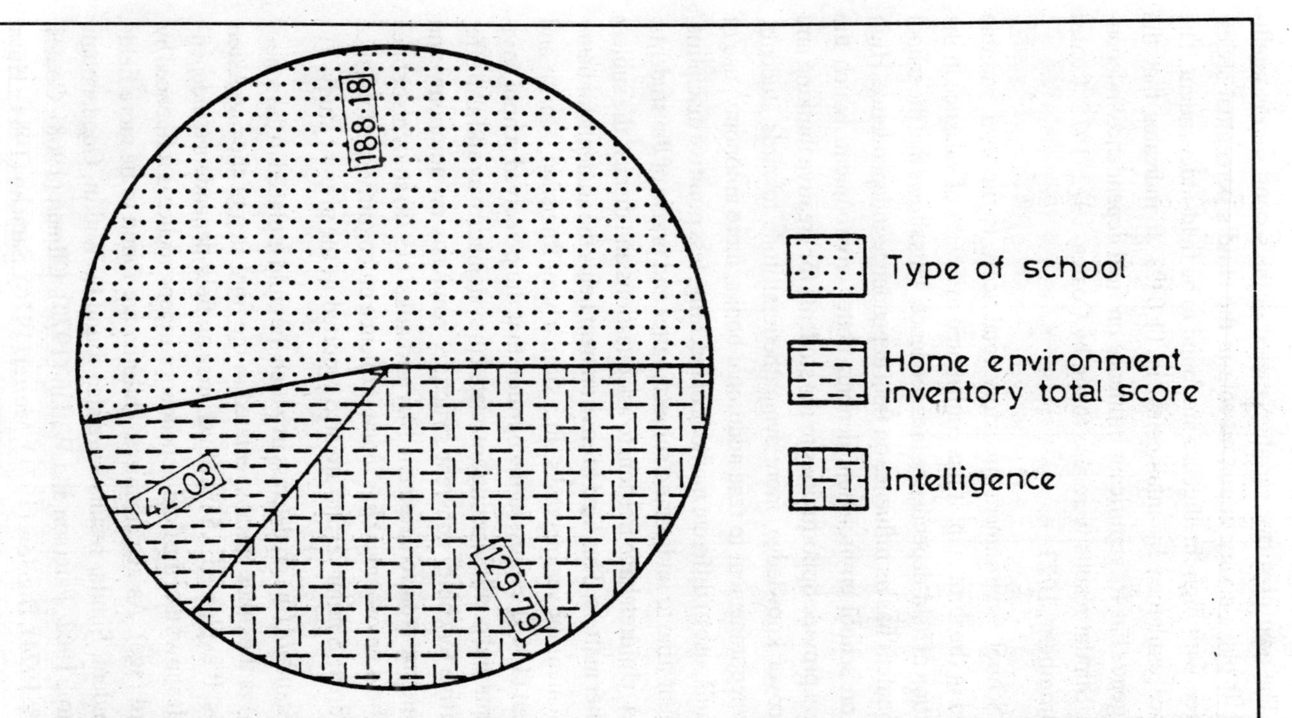

Fig. 5.7 : Relative Contribution (percentage) from independent variables to dependent variable—Perceptual Styles—Reflectivity/Impulsivity

The next predictor variable entered in the second step is intelligence. It plays a very important role in the child's perceptual styles. Children with high intelligence are found to be field-independent. The variance explained by intelligence is 11.04%. It indicates that the intelligence has its significant influence on field dependence/independence. Similar results were also found by Coates, 1972, 1975; Coates and Bromberg, 1973.

School environment inventory total score is the next variable entered in the third step. It has contributed to 5.93% of variance in the prediction offield-dependence/independence. This shows that the school environment has its influence on field dependence/independence. High score on school environment denotes better environment, which the teachers provide opportunities to the students for creative thinking and to discover knowledge, more sympathetic attitude towards students, more encouragement to read additional books, more autonomy, use of more aids, use of different methods of teaching, less punitive discipline, sufficient time to understand subject matter and praise of the students. Further, children have freedom to ask questions and discuss the subject and other matters. This kind of environment helps the students for better achievement on various tasks. In a similar way Ramsden, Martin and Bowden (1989) expressed the opinion that the perceived school environments and pupils learning are related in systematic way and also offer supportive teaching, coherent structure, emphasis on autonomy and moderate stress on achievement. Marjoribanks' (1978) study also states that school environment has much influence on cognitive performance in children. Similar results are also reported in the present study.

Standard (the grade/class in which the child is placed in the school system) is the other variable entered in the final step of the regression analysis. It explained 1.54% of variance on field-dependence/independence. It shows that the field-dependence/independence is influenced by standard (age). As age advances, children are found to be more field-independent. Similar results were also found by Witkin, Goodenough and Karp, 1967; Faterson and Witkin (1970), Oltman (1968), Coates (1972 & 1974), Bigelow (1971), Morrel (1976), Saracho (1984), Huss and Kayson (1985), Bill (1987), Kalyan Masih (1987) and Curry (1987).

Reflectivity/Impulsivity

With regard to the reflectivity/impulsivity, the type of school is entered as the first step in the regression analysis. It has contributed to the extend of 5.06% of variance on reflectivity/impulsivity. It is observed that private school children are found to be more reflective than quasi-government school children as indicated by the scores. In the private schools teacher encourage and stimulate the children to participate in various activities of the school and they also insist on their doing certain activities (curricular and extra curricular). It would foster child's cognitive development.

The next predictor variable entered in the second step was home environment inventory total score (HEIT). It has a very important role to play in child's perceptual development, HEIT explained for 1.13% of variance on reflectivity/impulsivity. High score on HEIT indicates better environment at home; where the parents provide more opportunities to understand things and situations and act according to their desires. Children receive maximum support and encouragement from parents. Children rarely receive punishment and have less restriction. This kind of environment helps the students for better performance on various tasks. Mar joribanks (1978) reported the significant influence of home environment on cognitive development and Sarala Paul (1987) found the influence of home on cognitive styles of children.

The next variable entered in the final step was intelligence. It has explained 3.49% of variance on reflectivity/impulsivity. Children with high intelligence are found to be more reflective and low intelligence appeared to be impulsive. These findings are in line with the results reported by Genser, Hafele and Hafele (1978), Brannigan, Ash and Margolis (1980), Miyakawa (1980) and Gjerde, Block and Block, 1985.

Salient Observations

The study is based on a sample of 240 children, selected from 8th,

9th and 10th standards of four schools located in Tirupati town. An equal number of boys and girls were selected from each standard both from private and quasi-government schools.

The analyses were confined to study the effects of home and school environment on perceptual styles of children. Further, an attempt was also made to study the effects of the demographic variables like type of school, standard, sex and intelligence on field-dependence/independence and reflectivity/impulsivity styles of children.

While looking into the composition of the children in respect of relative predominance of perceptual styles based on cut-off points of the score distribution, the following points can be recorded.

There is a greater proportion of field-dependent and impulsive children than field-independent and reflective.

χ^2 test revealed the significant association between field-dependence/independence and reflectivity/impulsivity ($\chi^2 = 9.052$, df = 1, $P < 0.5$). Several investigators reported that the reflectives are significantly more filed-independent (Campbell and Douglas, 1972; Koegh and Donlon, 1972; Massari and Massari, 1973; Mumbauer and Miller, 1972; Neimark, 1975; Schleifer and Douglas, 1983). The results of the present study are in line with the above findings.

The scores for private school children are relatively higher in both home and school environment than quasi-government school children. It is not surprising in the light of the discussion already made with regard to the difference between private and quasi-government schools.

With regard to availability, opportunity and utilization scores, private school children obtained higher scores than quasi-government school children.

The scores on RPM revealed marked differences in the level of intellectual functioning between the children of private and quasi-government schools.

The results also revealed that private school children tend to be field independent and reflective, whereas quasi-government school children are field-dependent and impulsive.

Significant age and sex differences are not observed with regard to field-dependence/independence and reflectivity/impulsivity styles.

The results of the multiple regression analyses revealed significant contribution of intelligence (RPM score), type of school, school environment and standard (age) on field-dependence/independence.

With regard to reflectivity/impulsivity style, type of school and home environment had significant influence.

Implications of the Study

There is some evidence in the study that the two perceptual styles chosen are influenced by intelligence (as measured by RPM), type of school and environment in home and school. A possible major implication, is whether the perceptual styles can be modified to improve the quality of information-processing and interactions with environment. What beneficial modifications are to be implemented in the present educational system to facilitate optimum cognitive development in children? Is it possible to achieve desirable modification in perceptual styles through specially designed games and exercises?. At least one thing seems to be certain, namely, the teachers and parents should be made to become aware of the existence of different perceptual styles in children and help the children to achieve better cognitive competence.

Role of Parents

Parents' and teachers' understanding and co-operation are necessary for smooth continuity of growth, as the child moves from home into a different environment at the school. This is important not only as the child enters kindergarten or nursery school but also as it moves back and forth between home and school throughout its formal educational experience (Breckenridge and Vincent, 1966). Generally parents in India think that their responsibilities cease when they send their children to school. They tend to feel that total responsibility to help them in their education lies with the teachers and the school. These days children are facing many problems in the present educational system. Until the child becomes self dependent parents should share the responsibilities to stimulate the children to learn good habits of reading, writing, spelling, thinking and problem-solving along with the teachers.

The findings of the study revealed that home and school environments are responsible for development of perceptual abilities in children. The findings of the investigation will help parents in deciding what type of environment should be created by them in their homes, so that their children will be able to develop their perceptual abilities to the maximum level. Parents should be given some guidance with regard to importance of different activities of children, encouragement, stimulation and their relationships with the children.

The child development specialists also should get involved in designing various cognitive oriented programmes and make the parents and teachers aware of these programmes.

Conclusions

The following are some of the salient conclusions drawn within the scope of the problem investigated.

1. Field-dependence/independence is significantly influenced by school environment.
2. Reflectivity/impulsivity is significantly influenced by home environment.
3. As the age increased the scores on field-dependence/independence also registered noticeable shift towards the higher level.
4. There are no significant sex differences in perceptual styles.
5. Children with high intelligence (fluid) tend to be more field-independent.
6. There is a need for creating awareness among parents and teachers regarding the existence of difference perceptual styles and their role in cognitive skills.

Methodological Limitations

The following are some of the methodological limitations.

1. The two tools HEI and SEI yielded an equivocal factorial structure. Items perhaps measuring more than one attribute in different areas are themselves overlapping. This aspect has to be looked into while refining the instruments.

2. The present investigation is mainly focussed on children of formal operational period. For comparison, studies may be conducted on various developmental periods.

3. In addition to RPM a verbal test would have given definitive information.

6

SUMMARY

Developmental trends in cognitive strategies to handle information in children are an important area of research. More specifically with the extensive build up of literature on the nature of perceptual styles, the interests got shifted to the investigation of specific perceptual styles and related phenomena.

Cross cultural data on the trends in the perceptual styles across different periods of growth and development are not well documented. The present study has attempted to investigate the effect of two important sources, namely, home and school environments upon the perceptual styles in children. The results of the study are expected to reveal within the home and school environments which may promote efficiency in the perceptual response system of the child and also to identify the specific components which may adversely influence.

Tools of Research

Home and school environments were measured by the two separate instruments. These instruments were adopted from the instruments constructed by Misra (1986). The basic psycho-metric properties were examined for these two instruments over a sample of 120. Item and factor analysis (with oblique rotations) were carried out to establish the influence of the tools. Home environment inventory Part A consisted of 45 items and Part B 36 items. These two parts measure psychosocial environment and physical aspects of the home environment. These 45 items were distributed over 7 factors. The split-half (odd-even) reliability of the home environment inventory was 0.79.

School environment inventory also consisted of Part A and B. Part A has 50 items while Part B 10 items. These 50 items were distributed over 8 factors. The split-half (odd-even) reliability of the SEI was 0.83.

The intellectual ability of the children was assessed by using Raven's Progressive Matrices (colour) Test.

The dependent variables, namely, the two perceptual styles, were assessed using Group Embedded Figure Test (Witkin, Raskin and Oltman, 1971) and Matching Familiar Figure Test (Developed on the basis of Kagan's model).

The Matching Familiar Figure Test was constructed based on theoretical model suggested by Kagan to measure reflectivity/impulsivity. This test consisted of 27 items which were very familiar to the children and also suitable to the local conditions. Pre-test was conducted over a sample of 30 and item analysis was carried out. Items having poor facility value of less than 2.85 were eliminated. Final booklet consisted of 24 items.

The following research questions were framed:

1. Is there any distribution bias in the quantitative measures of perceptual styles in sample children?
2. Is there any relationship between perceptual style and quality of environment?
3. Is there any association between age and perceptual styles?
4. Do these perceptual styles exhibit any dependencies on sex?
5. How does intelligence relate itself to the perceptual styles?

Sample

Two hundred and forty children studying 8th, 9th and 10th

standards of four schools in Tirupati town, Andhra Pradesh, India, constituted the sample of children for the study. The children were selected to represent educational level and sex from the pupils in the schools.

Analysis

The data obtained on a sample of 240 was statistically analysed to evaluate the significant contribution that each relevant independent variable makes to the two types of perceptual styles: field-dependence/independence and reflectivity/impulsivity. For this, two series of step-wise multiple regression analyses was done. In the first series field-dependence/ independence was treated as dependent variable. The home environment, school environment total score, type of school, standard, sex and intelligence were the independent variables.

In the second series reflectivity/impulsivity was the dependent variable and the home environment inventory, school environment inventory, total score, type of school, standard, sex and intelligence were independent variables.

The following are some of the major findings of the study.

1. School environment had its significant influence on the field-dependence/independence perceptual style.
2. Home environment is significantly associated with reflectivity/impulsivity.
3. As the age increased the scores on field-dependence/independence also registered noticeable shift towards the higher level.
4. There are no sex differences in perceptual styles - field-dependence/independence and reflectivity/impulsivity.
5. Intelligence had significant influence on field-dependence/independence.

There is a need for emphasizing training in cognitive skills through appropriate perceptual exercises for helping children to improve their cognitive abilities.

Most of the programmes in school are heavily loaded with information content rather than cognitive (perceptual) and reasoning skills. Therefore there is a need to review and modify the programmes in schools.

BIBLIOGRAPHY

Adams, W. (1972). Strategy differences between reflectives and impulsive children, *Child Development*, 43, 1076-1080.

Albert, N. B. B., and Howard, S. (1977). A cross-cultural investigation of child rearing and socioeconomic antecedents of field-dependence-independence, *Journal of Psychology*, 96, 63-70.

Annidon, E.J., and Flanders, N.A. (1961). The effects of direct and indirect teacher influence on dependent prone students learning geometry, *Journal of Educational Psychology*, 52, 286-291.

Anderson, G.J. (1970). Effects of class room social climate on individual learning, *Journal of American Educational Research*, 7, 135-152.

Anderson, G.J. (1971). Effect of course content and teacher sex on the social climate of learning. *Journal of American Educational Research*, 8, 649-663.

Angenent, H.L. (1976). The basis for child-rearing as determined by a questionnaire, *Psychological Abstracts*, 56(5), 934 (7787).

Armentrout, J.A. (1975). Repression-sensitization and MMP correlates of retrospective reports of parental child rearing behaviours,

Journal of Clinical Psychology, 31, 444–448.

Arrington, H.J. (1989). An investigation of the relationships between cognitive style, visualization and problem solving in eighth grade males and females, *Dissertation Abstracts International*, 49, 2151-A.

Ault, R.I., Mitchell, C., and Hartmann, D.P. (1975). Some methodological problems in reflection-impulsivity research, *Child Development, 47*, 227-231.

Baldwin, A.L., Kalhorn, J., and Breese, F.H. (1958). Patterns of parent behaviour, *Psychological Monograph*, 3(1), 73.

Barclay, A., and Cusumano, D.R. (1967) Father absence, cross-sex identity, and field-dependent behaviour in male adolescents, *Child Development*, 38, 243-250.

Becker, L.D., Bender, N.N., and Morrison, G. (1978). Measuring impulsivity reflection: A critical review, *Journal of Learning Disabilities*, *11*, 626-632.

Bertini, M., Pizzamiglio, L., and Wapner, S. (1986). *Field-dependence in Psychological Theory, Research and Application*, Lawrence Erlbaum Associates, INC, Hillsdale, New Jersey, London.

Bahal, M., and Sexena, V. (1978). Effects of family setting upon cognitive development of the children, *Child Psychology Quarterly*, *11*, 1-5.

Bhatnagar, A.B. (1977). Construction and standardisation of the treatment environment inventory, *Educational Trends, 12 (1,2)* 47-56.

Bigelow, G.S. (1971). Field dependence-field independence in 5 to 10 years old children, *Journal of Educational Research, 64(9)*, 393-400.

Bill, M. (1987). An examination of developmental trends in field-dependence among age groups of 10-21 years of age, *Perceptual Motor Skills, 64*, 117-118.

Block, J., and Block, J.H. (1973). *Ego development and the provenance of thought, NIMH Progress Report* (Grant No.M.H. 16080), University of California, Berkeley.

Block, J., and Block, J.H., and Harrington, D.M. (1974) Some misgivings about the matching familiar figures test as a measure of reflection impulsivity, *Developmental Psychology, 10*, 611-932.

Brdley, R.H. (1981). Preschool home environment and class room behaviour, *The Journal ofExperimental Education, 49*, 196-206.

Brannigan, G.G., Ash, T., and Margolis, H. (1980). Impulsivity-Reflectivity and children's intellectual performance, *Journal of Personality Assessment, 44*, 41-43.

Breckenridge, M.E. and Vincent, E.L., (1966). *Child development*, Tokyo, Toppan Company.

Brodzinsky, D.M. (1975). The role of conceptual tempo and stimulus characteristics in children's Humour development, *Developmental Psychology, 11*, 843-850.

Bronfenbrenner, U. (1961). Toward a theoretical model for the analysis of parent-child relationships in a social context, In Glidewell, J.C. (Ed)., *Parental attitudes and child behaviour*, Spring Feld , III: Thomas.

Bronfenbrenner, U. (1979). *The Ecology of Human Development*, Cambridge, mass, Harwar, U.P.

Bruner, J.S. (1962). The conditions of creativity, In Gruber, H., Terrel, G. and Wertheimer, M. (eds) *Contemporary approaches to creative thinking*, New Jersey E. Cliffs: Prentice Hall.

Campbell, S.B. (1973). Cognitive styles in reflective, impulsive and hyperactive boys and their mothers, *Perceptual and Motor Skills, 36*, 742-752.

Campbell, S.B., & Douglas, V.I. (1972). Cognitive styles and responses to the threat of frustration, *Canadian Journal of Behavioural Science, 4*, 30-42.

Carolina, U., and Greenville, N.C. (1988). Field-independence and simultaneous processing in Pre-school Children, *Perceptual & Motor Skills, 66 (3)*, 891-897.

Carter, H., and Loo, R. (1980). Group embedded figures test: Psychometric data, *Perceptual and Motor Skills, 50*, 32-34.

Cattell, R.B. (1963). Theory of Fluid and crystallized intelligence: A critical experiment, *Journal of Educational Psychology, 54*, 1-22.

Coates, S. (1972). *Pre-school embedded figure test*, Palo Alto, California: Consulting Psychologists Press.

Coates, S. and Bromberg, P.M. (1973). The factorical structure of the WPPSI between the ages of 4 and 6, *Journal of consulting and Clinical Psychology, 40*, 356-370.

Coates, S. (1974a). Sex differences in field independence among preschool children. In R.C. Friedman, R.M. Richart, & R.L. Vande Wiele (Eds). *Sex differences in behaviour*, New Yourk, Wiley.

Coates, S. (1974b). Sex differences in field dependence-independence between the ages of 3 and 6, *Perceptual and Motor Skills*, 39, 1307-1310.

Coates, S. (1975). Field-dependence and intellectual functioning in preschool children, *Perceptual and Motor Skills*, 41, 251-254.

Cogan, M.L. (1964). The relation of the behaviour of teachers to the productive behaviour of their pupils, Unpublished doc+oral dissertation, Harward University.

Cohen J. (1979). Patterns of Parental help, *Educational Research, 21*, 196-193.

Crandall, V., Preston, A., and Rabson, A. (1960). Maternal reactions and the development of independence and achievement behaviour in young children, *Child Development, 31*, 243-251.

Crandall, V., Katkovsky, W., and Preston, A.A. (1960). A conceptual formulation for some research-children's achievement development, *Child Development, 31*, 243-251.

Daini, S., and Bertini, M. (1979). Some cultural influences on cognitive styles, *Journal of Psychology, 16(3)*, 225-235.

Dave, R.H. The identification and measurement of environment process variables that are related to educational achievement, Ph. D. thesis, University of Chicago, cited by Marjoribanks, K. in Environment as threshold variable: an examination, *Journal of Educational Research, 1974, 67 (5)*, 210-212.

Dermen, D., and Meissner, J.A. (1972). Pre-school embedded figures test. In V.C. Shipman (Ed), *Disadvantaged children and their first school experiences*. (PR-72-27) Princeton, New Jersey: Educational Testing Service.

Egeland, B. (1974). Training impulsive children in the use of more efficient scanning techniques, *Child Development, 45*, 165-171.

Ehman, L.H. (1970). A comparison of three sources of class room data: Teachers, studetns and systematic observation. Paper presented at the meeting of the *American Educational Research Association*, Minneapolis.

Elardo, R., Bradley, R., and Caldwell, B.M. (1975). The relation of infants home environments to mental test performance from six to thirty six months, *Child Development*, *46*, 71-76.

Engle, P., Klein, R., Kagan, J., and Yarbrough, C.K. (1977). Cognitive performance during middle childhood in,rural Guatemala, *Journal of General Psychology, 131*, 291-307.

Epstein, J.L., and Mc Partland, J.M. (1976). Class room organization and quality of school life, *Centre of social organisation of school reports,* John Hopkins University, 215-235.

Faterson, H.F., and Witkin, H.A. (1970). Longitudinal study of development of body concept, *Developmental Psychology*, *2*, 429-438.

Flanders, N.A. (1951). Personal- scoial anxiety as a factor in experimental learnign situations, *Journal of Educational Research, 45*, 100-110.

Flexer, B.K., and Roberge, J.J. (1980). Field-dependence-independence and the development of formal operational thought, *Journal of General Psychology, 103*, 191-201.

Garrett, H.E. (1981). *Statistics in psychology and education*, Vakils, Feffer and Simons Ltd., Bombay.

Genser, B., Hafele, A., and Hafele, M. (1978). Reflection and impulsivity: Ability or cognitive style, *Psychologie*, 10,114-123.

Ghuman, P.A. (1980). A comparative study of cognitive styls in three ethnic groups, *International Review of Applied Psychology, 29*, 75-87.

Gjerde, P.F., Block, J., and Block, J.H. (1985). Longitudinal consistency of matching familiar figurs test performance from early child hood to preadolescence, *Developmental Psychology, 21(2)*, 262-227.

Goldberg, J.B. (1968). Influence of pupils' attitudes on perception of teachers' behaviours and on consequent school work, *Journal of Educational Psychology, 59*, 1-15.

Goldstein, H.S., and Peck, R. (1973). Maternal differentiation, father absence and cognitive differentiation in children, *Archs Gen. Psychiat. 29*, 370-373.

Grebow, H. (1973). The relationship of some parental variables to achievement and values in college women, *Journal of Educational Research, 66(5)*, 203-209.

Halpin, G., and Peterson, H. (1986). Accommodation instructions to learners field independence/dependence: A study of effects on achievement and attitudes, *Perceptual motor skills, 62*, 967-974.

Hall, D.T. (1970). The effects of teacher student cogruence upon student learning in college classes, *Journal of Educational Psychology, 61(3)*, 205-213.

Heider, E.R. (1971). Information processing and the modification of an "impulsive conceptual tempo". *Child Development, 42*, 1276-1281.

Heider, E.R. (1971). "Focal" colour areas and development of colour names, *Developmental Psychology, 4*, 447-455.

Helen, M., Walt, B., and Clifford, H.A. (1987). Cognitive learning style and achievement in mathematics, *Journal of Instructional Psychology, 14(1)*, 26-28.

Hughes, R.N. (1978). Sex differences in field-dependence, effects of unlimited time on group embedded figures test performance, *Perceptual and motor skills, 47*, 1246.

Hunt, D.E., and Sullivan, E.V. (1974). Between psychology and education, Illinois, Hinsdale: Dryden Press, 84-101.

Huss, ET., and Kayson, W.A. (1985). Effects of age, sex on speed of founding embedded figures, *Perceptual and motor skills, 61*, 591-594.

Johnson, R.C., and Medinnus, G.H. (1969). *Child psychology: Behaviour and development*, New York, John Wiley and Sons.

Juliano, D.B. (1977). Reflection – impulsivity and concept learning in disadvantaged and middle class children, *Journal of Pscyhology, 96*, 103-110.

Kagan, J., Rosman, B.L., and Day, D., Albert, J., and Phillips, W. (1964). Information processing in the child significance of analytic and reflective attitudes, *Psychological Monographis, 78*, 1-37.

Kagan, J. (1965). Impulsive and reflective children: Significance of conceptual tempo, In J.D. Krumboltz (Ed.), *Learning and the Educational Process*, Chicago: Rand McNally.

Kagan, J. (1965). Reflection-impulsivity and reading **ability** in primary grade children, *Child Development, 36*, 609-628.

Kagan, J. (1965). Individual differences in the resolution of response uncertainty, *Journal of Personality and Social Psychology, 2*, 154-160.

Kagan, J., and Kogan, N. (1970). Individual variation in cognitive processes. In P. Mussen (Ed.) *Carmichael's Manual of child psychology, 1*, New York: Wiley.

Kagan, J., and Messer, S.B. (1975). A reply to some misgivings about the matching Familiar Figures Test as a measure of reflection-impulsivity, *Developmental Psychology, 11*, 244-248.

Kalyani Devi, T. (1982). Effects of age, sex and environmental deprivation on the performance of pre-school children on simple perceptual tasks, *M. Phil. Dissertation* submitted to Sri Venkateswara University, Tirupati.

Kalyan - Masih, V., and Curry (1987). Cognitive performance and cognitive style of young children, *Perceptual and motor skills, 65 (2)*, 571- 579.

Karp, S.A., and Konstadt, N.L. (1963). *Manual for the children's embedded figure test*, Brooklyn, New York: Cognitive tests.

Koegh, B.K., and Donlon, G. (1972). Field dependence, impulsivity and learning disabilities, *Journal of Learning Disabilities, 5*, 331-336.

Kogan, N. (1976). *Cognitive styles in infancy and early childhood,* Lawrnce Erlbaum Associates Publishers, Hillsdale, New Jersey.

Kogan, N. (1976). Sex differences in creativity and cognitive styles, In S.Messick (Ed), *Individuality in learning: cognitive styles and creativity for human development,* Sanfrancisoc: Jossey - Bass.

Lawry, J. A., and Welsh, M.C., and Jeffrey, W.E. (1983). Cognitive tempo and complex problme solving, *Child Development, 54,* 912-920.

Lorr, M., and Jenkins, R.L. (1953). Three factors in parent behaviour, *Journal of Consulting Psychology, 17*, 306-308.

Majeed, A., and Ghosh, E.S.K. (1983). Effects of ethnicity; social class and residential background on cognitive differentiation, *Psychological Studies, 28,* 13-17.

Majoribanks, K. (1978). Personality and environmental correlates of cognitive performance and school elated affective characteristics: A regression surface analysis, *Journal of Educational Research, 24*, 230-243.

Majoribanks, K. (1981). School psychology and family environment research: A frame work for analysis, *Psychological Abstracts, 68,* 97.

Massari, D.J., and Massari, J.A. (1973). Sex differences in the relationship of cognitive style and intellectual functioning in disadvantaged preschool children, *Journal of Genetic Psychology, 122,* 175-181.

Messer, S. (1970). The effect of anxiety over intellectual performance on reflection impulsivity in children, *Child Development, 40,* 785-797.

Messer, S.B. (1976). Reflection-impulsivity: A review, *Psychological Bulletin, 83,* 1026-1052.

Messer, S.B., and Brodzinsky, D.M. (1981). Three year stability of reflection impulsivity in young adolescents, *Developmental psychology, 17,* 848-850.

Misra, K.S. (1986). *Effect of home and school environments on scientific creativity*, Academy Press, Allahabad.

Mitchell, J.V. (1963). Self-family perceptions related to self acceptance manifest anxiety and neuroticism, *Journal of Educational Research, 56*, 236.

Miyakawa, J. (1980). The response flexibility in cognitively-impulsive children, *Japanese Journal of Psychology, 51(3),* 164-167.

Moos, R. (1974). *Evaluating treatment environment: A social ecological approach.* New York: John Weley and Sons.

Moos, R.H., and Trickett, E.J. (1974). Class room environment scale manual, Palo Alto: Consulting Psychologist Press. Quoted by Nielson, D.H. and Moos, R.H. in Exploration and adjustment in high school class rooms- A study of person-environment fit, *Journal of Educational Research, 1978, 72(1)*, 52-57.

Moss and Belins. (1986). *Hand Book of Stress*, 212-230, conceptualising in Leo Goldberger and Shlome, Brezintz, Free Press.

Morell, J. (1976). Age, sex, training and the measurement of field-dependence, *Journal of Experimental Child Psychology, 22*, 100-112.

Mumbauer, C.C.,and Miller, J.O. (1972). Socio-economic background and cognitive functioning in pre-school children, *Child Development, 41*, 471-480.

Neimark, E.D. (1975). Longitudinal development of formal operations thought, *Genetic Psychology Monogrpahs, 91*, 171-225.

Okanji, O. M. (1969). The differential effects of rural and urban upbringing on the development of cognitive styles, *International Journal of Psychology, 4*, 293-305.

Olson, D.R. (1970). *Cognitive development: The child's aquisition of diagonality*, New York, Academic Press.

Oltman, P.K. (1968). Portable rod - and - frame apparatus, *Perceptual and motor skills, 26*, 503-506.

Oltman, P.K., Raskin, E., and Witkin, H.A. (1971). *Group Embedded Figure Test*, Consulting psychologists Press, Inc. Palo Alto, California.

Perkin, H.V. (1951). Climate influences group learning, *Journal of Educational Resarch, 45*, 115-119, 48.

Perny, V.H. (1976). Effects of race and sex on field-dependence/ Independence in children, *Perceptual and Motor Skills, 42*, 975–980.

Piaget, J. (1967). *Six psychological studies*, New York, Random House.

Pumroy, D.K. (1966). Mary Land parent attitude survey: A reserch instrument with social desirability controlled, *Journal of Psychology, 64*, 73-78.

Ramsden, P., Martin, E., and Bowden, J. (1989). School Environment and Sixth Form Pupils', Approaches to learning, *British Journal of Educational Psychology, 59*, 129-142.

Rath, S. (1992). Cognitive behaviour intervention with disadvantaged tribal school children: An empirical study, *Indian Journal of Clinical Psychology, 19(1)*, 4-9.

Roven, J.C. (1987). *Coloured progressive matrices*, published by Manasayan, New Delhi, J.C. Raven Ltd.

Resendiz, P.S.C., and Fox R.A. (1985). Reflection-impulsivity in Mexican Children Cross cultural relationships, *Journal of General Psychology, 112*, 285-290.

Rogers, R.(1967). *Cornel parent behaviour description, College of Human Development*, Cornell University, Ithaka.

Rosen, B., and D'Andrade, R. (1959). The psychological origins of achievement motivation, *Sociometry, 22*, 185-218.

Roth, R.M. (1961). *Manual for the Mother-child relationship evaluation*, Western Psychological Services, Los Angles

Salkind, N.J., and Wright, J.C. (1977). The development of reflection-impulsivity and cognitive efficiency, *Hunan Development, 20*, 377-387.

Salkind, N.L., and Nelson, C.F., (1980). A note on the geometrical nature of reflection impulsivity, *Developmental psychology, 16*, 237-238.

Saracho, O.N. (1984). Young children's academic achievement as a function of their cognitive styles, *Journal of Research Development in Education, 18(1)*, 44-50.

Sarala Paul, (1987). A study of cognitive styles of high school students of Home Science in relation to age, achievement, home environment and social class, *Indian Dissertation Abstracts, 16,* 347-349.

Scheck, D.C., and Emerick, R.C. (1976). The young male adolescents perception of early child-rearing behaviour: The differential effects of socio-economic status and family size, *Sociometry, 39* 39-52.

Schleifer, M.,and Douglas, V.I. (1973). Moral judgements, behaviour and cognitive style in young children, *Canadian Journal of Behavioural Science, 5,* 113-114.

Schwebel, A. (1966). Effects of impusivity on performance of verbal tasks in middle and lower class children, *American Journal of Orthopsychiatry, 36,* 12-21.

Sharma, H.C., and Chouhan, N.S. (1980). *Manual for parent child relatinship scale,* National Psychological Corporation, Agra.

Sigel, I.E., and Brodzinsky, D.M. (1977). Individual differences: A perspective for understanding intellectual developement. In H.L.Home and P.A. Rabinsons (Eds.), *Psychological Process in early education*, New York, Academic Press.

Sigelman, E. (1969). Reflective and impulsive observing behaviour, *Child Development, 40,* 1213-1222.

Silbergeld, S., Koenig, C.R. and Manderscheid, R.W., (1975). Classroom psychological environment, *Journal of Educational Research, 69*, 151-155.

Sinha, D. (1984),*Manual for story- Pictorial, E.F.T. and Indo-African E.F.T.,* Varanasi, Rupa Psychological Centre.

Smith, J.D., and Caplan, J., (1988).Cultural differences in cognitive style development, *Developmental Psychology, 24(1),* 46-52.

Solis- Camara, P.R., and Gomez Matha, L. (1985) Children's human figure drawings and impulsvie style of two levels of socio-economic status, *Perceptual and motor skills, 61*, 1039-1042.

Srivastave, A.K. (1989). A study on field-dependence-independence among Mizo children, *Psychological studies, 34(1)*, 55-58.

Steele, J.M., House, E.R. and Kerins, T. (1971). An instrument for assessing instructional climate through low inference student judgement, *American Educational Research Journal, 8*, 447-466.

Swinnen, S. Vandenberghe, J., and Van Assche, E. (1986). Role of cognitive style constructs field-dependence-independence and reflectivity-impulsivity in skill acquistition, *Journal of Sports Psychology*, 8, 51-69.

Symonds, P.M. (1939). *The psychology of parent-child relatinship*, New York, Appleton Century Crofts.

Tharakan, P.N.O. (1987). The effect of rural and urban upbringing on cognitive styles, *Psychological Studies, 12(7)*, 119-122.

Thomas, S.A.W. (1971). The role of cognitive style variables in mediating the influence of aggressive television upon elementary school children, unpublished doctoral dissertation, University of California, Los Angles.

Verma, B.P.(1991). A study of the cognitive style with anxiety and academic achievement, *Journal of Education and Psychology, XXXXVIII, No.3-4*, Oct/Jan, 156-161.

Walberg, H.J. (1969). Social environment as a mediatory of class room learning, *Journal of Educational Psychology, 60*, 443-448.

Ward, W.C. (1968). Reflection-impulsivity in Kindergarten children, *Child Development, 39*, 867-874.

Ward, W.C.(1973). *Correlates and implications of self regularity behaviours*. (PR-73-42) Princeton, New Jersey: Educational Testing Service.

Watson, G. (1957). Some personality diferences in children related to strict or permissive parental discipline, *Journal of Psychology, 44*, 227-249.

Weintraub, S.A. (1973). Self-control as a correlate of an internalizing-externalizing symptom dimension, *Journal of Abnromal Child psychology, 1*, 292-307.

William, R.M. and Wilson, R.C. (1961). Family relations of bright high-achieving and under achieving high school boys, *Child Development, 32*, 501-510.

Winterbottom, M. (1958). The relation of need for achievement in learning experience in independence and mastery. In atkinson, J. (Ed). *Motives in fantasy action and society*, Princeton, N.J: Van Nostrand, 453-478.

Witkin, H.A. (1954). Personality through perception, New York, Harper.

Witkin, H.A. (1962). The problem of individuality in development. In S. Wapner and B.Kaplan (Eds). *Perspectives in Psychological Theory* (pp 335-361), New Yourk, International Universities press.

Witkin. H.A., Dyk, R.B., FAterson, H.F., Goodenough, D.R. and Karp, S.A. (1962). *Psychological differentation*, New York, Wiley.

Witkin, H.A., and Oltman, P.K. (1967). Cognitive style, *International Journal of Neurology, 6*, 119-137.

Witkin, H.A., Goodenough, D.R., & Karp, S.A., (1967). Stability of cognitive style from childhood to young adulthood, *Journal of personality and Social Psychology*, 7, 291-300.

Witkin, H.A., Prince-Williams, D., Bertini, M., Christiansen, B., Oltman, P.K., Ranmdrez, M., and Van Meel, J. (1974). Social conformity and psychological differentiation, *International Journal of Psychology, 9*, 11-29.

Witkin, H.A., and Goodenough, D.R., (1977). Field-dependence and interpersonal behaviour, *Psychological Bulletin, 84*, 661–689.

Witkin, H.A. (1979). Socialization, culture and ecology in the development of group and sex differences in cognitive style, *Human Development, 22*, 358-372.

Witkin, H.A., Goodenough, D.R., and Oltman, P.K. (1979). Psychological differentiation: current status, *Journal of Personality and Social Psychology, 37*, 1127-1145. (Also ETS Research Bulletin 77-17, 1977).

Wober, M. (1967). Adapting Witkin's field-independence theory to accommodate new information from Africa, *British Journal of Psychology, 58*, 29-38.

Wohlford, P., and Liberman, D. (1970). Effect of father absence on personal time, field-independence and anxiety, *Proc, 78th Ann Convention, American psychological Association*, 263-264.

Yardo, R.M., and Kagan, J. (1968). The effect of teacher tempo on the child. *Child Development, 39*, 27-34.

Zilniker, T., and Jeffrey, W.E. (1976). Reflective and impulsive children; strategies for information processing underlying differences in problem-solving, *Monographs of the society for Research in Child Development*, 41.

Zucker, J., and Stricker, G.(1968). Impulsivity reflectivity in pre-school head-start and middle class children, *Journal of Learning Disabilities, 1*, 24-30.

—

INDEX